Fork in the Road

...and other pointless discussions

Other Books by Linda M. Au

Humor:

Head in the Sand . . . and other unpopular positions
Train of Thought: Travel Essays from a One-Track Mind
Travel Documents

Novels:

Secret Agent Manny
The Scarlet Letter Opener (Red Ink Mystery #1)
The Tell-Tale Heart Attack (Red Ink Mystery #2)
Charlotte's Website (Red Ink Mystery #3)
Gray Area

with a foreword by James Watkins

ISBN: 978-1-954973-04-6

Visit Linda online:
lindaau.com

Follow Linda on Twitter:
@LindaMAu

Stalk Linda on Facebook:
facebook.com/AuthorLindaMAu/

Cover design by Rosamond Grupp
Cover artwork by Mike Ferrin / mikeferrin.org

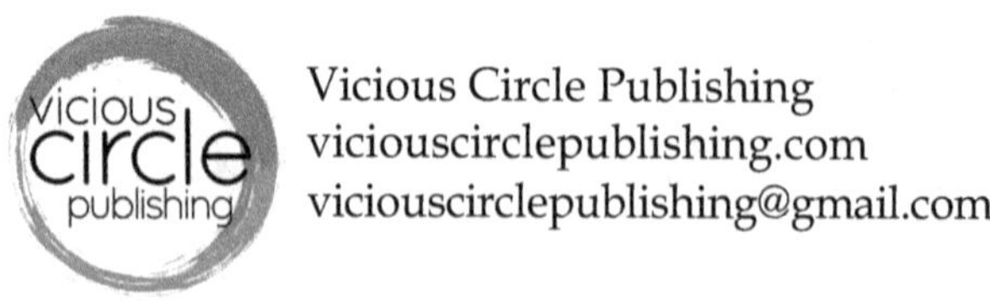

Vicious Circle Publishing
viciouscirclepublishing.com
viciouscirclepublishing@gmail.com

For Wayne,
who may read this someday . . .
when he's done working overtime

For my parents,
who will read this the second it's out . . .
and laugh like crazy because they know
their parenting skills improve with age

Table of Cutlery … I mean, Contents

Acknowledgments

Thanks go to my "beta testers," who did a lot of email-hand-holding while I wrung my hands over titles, subtitles, cover design issues, word choices, and photographs. Without these folks answering frantic emails from me with subject lines such as, "Wait, not that one, THIS one!" and "No no no, I sent the wrong file ... again!," I would never have gotten this book to print.

Some days it just doesn't pay to do your own project management, even if you've done it for a living for decades. Thanks, guys!

Chris Bowyer (*who wishes to be known as Alan Smithee*)

Lynne Gordon

Jerry Hatchett

Dora Machado

Lisa McClinsey

Fara Howell Pienkosky

Mel Rigney

Foreword

I have in my right hand, direct from my home office in Corn Borer, Indiana, today's category:

Top Ten Reasons to Buy Linda Au's Latest Book

10. I actually LOLed reading Linda's book. Okay, maybe not ROFL or laughing off parts of my body, but I did LOL and you will too.

9. I've written a textbook on humor writing, *Writing with Banana Peels,* and teach a class on the subject at Taylor University and at conferences. So, I know a bit about what makes writing funny, and I can certify Linda is truly funny. (She is indeed certifiable!)

8. Since the Good Book claims humor is a good medicine, Linda's book is sure to cure what ails you. (Warning from Linda's humor-impaired lawyer: The Federal Drug Administration has not approved this book for the treatment of any ailments, conditions, or syndromes advertised on the evening news, nor does the publisher make any claims—overt or implied—of the medical benefits of this book. Do not read while operating heavy machinery. If laughter lasts more than four hours, seek immediate medical attention.)

7. University studies, however, have proven that laughter does increase dopamine production in the brain, creating a perfectly safe and legal "high" similar to sex, drugs, and rock and roll. And without unpleasant child support payments, hangovers, or hearing loss!

6. It makes the perfect gift for the person who has everything. And, besides, who needs a genuine, limited-edition, non-operable replica of a *Star Wars* light saber (batteries not included), ermine golf club covers, or any of the other high-priced stuff he or she doesn't need in those specialty catalogs. What they really need is a good laugh—and Linda delivers!

5. If you buy a case of *Fork in the Road* (shipping not included), Linda will phone you on your birthday and sing a selection of Broadway tunes. For five cases, she will speak at your church, conference, or convenience store grand opening. And for ten cases, Linda will donate a kidney. (This is a one-time offer!)

4. Linda promised me a free book if I said nice things about *Fork in the Road*.

3. If you don't buy this book in huge quantities, Linda will be forced to go on government assistance. So, you're actually further ahead paying the cover price than supporting her as she stands on the corner with a cardboard sign: "Will Write for Food."

2. Linda has a way of taking ordinary things—squirrels, weed whackers, DIY projects, waterbeds, and head wounds—and mining the humor out of them. She's a fracking genius.

1. After reading Linda's madcap adventures, you'll be able to smugly boast, "I'm not half as nutty as that crazy woman!"

Seriously (Can you say that in a humor book?!), I love Linda's humor on the page and in person. She is one of the funniest people I know who is still allowed out in public without professional supervision. You're going to LOL!

James Watkins: author, speaker, threat to society
www.jameswatkins.com
www.hopeandhumor.org

Introduction

I don't have to think up clever, original, funny things in order to write humor. I just have to pay attention and remember to write things down before I forget them. Especially at my age. If I didn't carry a little black notebook in my purse or keep a digital voice recorder in my car, this book wouldn't exist. Remembering tomorrow why something is funny today is like trying to remember a dream more than ten minutes after I wake up. If I don't write it down within minutes, it's gone forever. Unless it's that dream where I'm singing songs from *Phantom of the Opera* in a clown suit before the elders of my church, accompanying myself on a poorly tuned ukulele. That dream never goes away, no matter how hard I try.

Once you can remember everything, humor becomes mostly a matter of perspective. Things that frustrate the heck out of most people will make me think, "Where's that little black notebook?" Things that make you want to hit somebody upside the head with a swizzle stick make me want to grab a word processor and jot it all down. People-watching becomes a source of amusement rather than a source of stalking (although sometimes the two overlap, and everybody knows restraining orders just aren't funny).

Making a conscious choice to find everything funny has not only led to a source of revenue from my humor books, but it also leads to a happier me the rest of the time when I'm not scribbling notes about people or writing down another strange thing my husband just did. Looking at the world through nosy-colored glasses is a wonderful way to go through life. I highly recommend it.

Because, if you can't laugh at yourself, well ... I'll laugh at you instead. And then I'll write it down when you're not looking.

Linda M. Au

June 2013

Driving Me Crazy

"The turn for Route 168 is right up here, dear."

"I know, Mom. I saw the sign back there. It's coming up on the left."

"Right. Now, slow down."

"Right? The sign said left. And, I'm going fifteen miles an hour in a forty zone. I'm fine."

"I meant, right, as in, yes, it's on the left. And, you're going to have to slow down if you don't want to fly around the corner."

"You meant, right, as in left? Mom, that doesn't make sense. And of course I don't want to fly around the corner. Which is why I'm now going ten miles an hour two blocks ahead of the intersection."

"It's only one block, and you're going to miss it if you don't—*oh no!*"

I slam on the brakes, taking us down to something like negative-two miles per hour.

"What?"

"I think I forgot my gloves."

"You yelled 'oh no!' in the middle of telling me how to drive just because you may have forgotten your gloves?"

"Yes, it's chilly outside. I might need those gloves."

"Mom, it's sixty degrees outside."

"But you've got the air-conditioning on in the car."

"No, I don't."

"Yes, you do. I feel a little chill."

She puts her hands over the vents in front of her, and I again wonder why I ever let her sit in the front seat. I can hear my dad in the back seat chuckling. He'd rather cram his knees into the back of my Cobalt than sit up front driving with my mom in the passenger seat. I realize I should never have felt sorry for him having to sit in the back alone. Right now I wouldn't mind sitting in the trunk with the spare tire and the two extra plastic bottles of wiper fluid.

"Mom, I don't have the air conditioning on, I swear."

I suppose I deserve this sort of abuse ever since I got the new car—you know, the one where the air conditioning actually works. I start cranking up the A/C sometime in late February in anticipation of the warm weather, despite the fact that I live in Pittsburgh and we have a history of blizzards during the St. Patrick's Day parade. I guess I just get a huge rush out of turning on the air conditioning after a long winter and finding that it actually still works.

So, this is a case of the girl who cried wolf. It's late March and it's sixty degrees outside and I swear I don't have the A/C on, but my mother knows me too well. At the very least, this is her subtle way of telling me not to turn the A/C on, although I've already told her she can play with the fan and heat panel on the dashboard all she wants while I'm driving.

"Mom, it's not cold in here. Plus, you're wearing your winter coat and a scarf and I'm wearing just a sweater. But if you're cold, you can adjust the heat right there in front of you."

"Remember, I'm from Las Vegas. I chill easily."

"Mom, you lived in Vegas for ten years out of seventy-one years. You're not 'from' Las Vegas."

"But we retired there, so it's the most recent ten years."

"No, it's not. You've lived back here in Pennsylvania for nearly eight years now. And it's sixty degrees."

My dad clears his throat from the back seat and speaks up. "You missed the turn. It was two blocks back on the left."

My mom and I both turn to glare at him.

"Shut up!" we yell in unison.

From the back seat I hear more chuckling.

Are we there yet?

No Sense of Humor

So, we're apparently house-hunting now. Wayne and I are so different in so many ways (he's an electrical engineer and I'm a writer—'nuf said) that I figure I should ask him what kinds of things he'll be looking for in a new house.

"Well, I like a two-story house."

Meanwhile, I was thinking a ranch house since we both just hit 50 and we ain't gettin' any younger.

"Okay, I suppose we could always install one of those chair-lift thingies when we get older," I say in a spirit of compromise. "What else?"

"And, I think it should be on a level lot."

"Aha, so it'll be easier to mow and take care of?"

"No, there's always a riding mower. I just thought

you could do more with a level lot."

"Such as...?"

"...Like, you know, parking junked-up cars there."

Silence.

More silence.

I look over and, after what is an agonizing ten more seconds, the dimples show up and he cracks a smile. I relax my tightened forehead and sphincter and breathe freely. You see, I've lived with this man for over a decade now. He could've been dead serious. I'm just relieved he sees fit to laugh at his own jokes, even if he never laughs at mine.

It's going to be a longggggg house hunt.

What's So Funny?

So, you think you're funny? You want to write humorous essays and collect them into a cute little book and make dozens and dozens of dollars? You think you've got it in you to wow the crowd with a Dave Barry homage that leaves your reader gasping for breath over your latest knee-slapper? (By the way, I've made people laugh my whole life, and I don't think I've ever seen anyone actually slap a knee in response. Maybe I'm doing it wrong.)

I'll be the first to admit, writing humor isn't rocket science. I'm not sure exactly what that means, except that even rocket science isn't even rocket science anymore now that NASA seems to have stopped making rockets. You know the economy is bad when rocket scientists are collecting unemployment like normal people. And besides, rocket science isn't very funny. Which is obvious if you've ever had to sit next to a rocket scientist at a dinner party. Which I haven't. I'm never invited to those kinds of parties. Not that I'm complaining, if only because of that whole rocket-science-isn't-funny thing.

Where was I? Oh, yeah, writing humor.

Although writing humor doesn't use much of either side of my brain—left brain, right brain, who can keep them straight anyway?—some days it's excruciatingly painful to write anything funny. On those days, it feels like I'm running the Pittsburgh marathon in the snow (don't laugh—this is Pittsburgh in the spring we're talking about*) in my bare feet, wearing a pair of my petite daughter's skinny jeans and a Pirates T-shirt dipped in ice water, carrying a watermelon on my head without using my hands. In fact, on *good* days that's what it feels like. And I don't have many of the good days.

Picture it: I dig out the mysterious little black notebook (which only seems mysterious until you look inside and find it's got doodles and scribbles on it like I'm still in junior high and practicing how to write my future married name for when the boy sitting next to me discovers I'm alive and falls crazy in love with me—*Mrs. Joe Schmoe ... Mrs. Linda Schmoe ... Mrs. Linda Au Schmoe ...*

---

* Wait, go ahead and laugh. I'm trying to be funny here.

Mr. and Mrs. Joseph Q. Schmoe … Joseph and Linda Schmoe request the honour of your presence ...). Then I stare at all these unfunny notes I've been keeping on every funny* incident that pops into my field of vision … and I start to weep uncontrollably.

Why do things that had me laughing so hard while I was driving that I veered off the road and nearly hit another squirrel (don't ask about the first squirrel—I'm still suffering from PTSD) now seem trite, ridiculous, and a lot more like fodder for a bad eulogy—for a person I didn't even like all that much? Where is that inspiration that carried me through so many humor writing contests over the years, only to land me here, alone in my office on a chair that's too short for this desk and a chair mat that must have a thin coating of Vaseline on it for all the success I'm having keeping the chair in one spot?

Where is the muse that coaxed me out of my shell long enough to get an entire first book of humor essays out of me, only to leave me stranded now that I'm on a serious deadline and wish I hadn't spent the past three weeks building an awesome underground cave in Minecraft instead? (It was a pretty awesome cave, though—water tumbling down one side, a huge dungeon at the bottom filled with storage chests brimming over with obsidian and redstone and—oops, never mind.)

Because seriously, even coming up with that bit about the skinny jeans and the watermelon on the pre-

* at the time

vious page was sheer torture. And admit it, it wasn't even all that funny.

I'd say this book is a true labor of love, but that would only be half right. The labor part is right. The love part, not so much. It's not like I get to sit here with a clown nose on my face playing Spike Jones records and tooting an air horn any time someone interrupts my train of thought. Most days I'm pretty sure that train has totally derailed. In reality, I usually sit here in my office at the old computer I use for writing (sitting at what I have secretly dubbed the Desk of Doom), staring at a line of how-to books on writing (mocking me, taunting me, *o! how they taunt me!*), and my Alfred E. Neuman "What—me worry?" statue, and a free promotional bobblehead of former replacement-level Pirate player Richie Zisk, who keeps nodding at me as if to egg me on. Nice try, Zisk. What do you know about writing humor? You never had better than a .287 batting average anyway. And only the other team ever found *that* funny.

Anyway, here I sit, staring at the computer screen, thinking I really should go clean the toilet with my toothbrush or declaw the neighbor's cat with a pair of tweezers or remodel our only remaining bathroom with one hand tied behind my back—anything to get away from this keyboard and its accusing silence.

O, the slings and arrows of outrageous jokes! I have become a slave of the pun, a servant of the double entendre, a master of pretty much nothing except making a really wicked cheeseburger pie, even if I just use the recipe on the side of the Bisquick box and modify it by taking out the few nourishing ingredients so my kids will actually eat it.

So I turn off the television. I silence the iPod. I pull down the shades. I await inspiration the way a dog waits to be let out in the pre-dawn morning darkness … and still nothing, still I am left whimpering by the back door, shaking uncontrollably with my legs crossed hoping some poor soul will take pity on me and let me out of this suffocating existence if I whine loudly enough and chew on the sofa.

And, before I know it, I've piddled on the carpet and pretty much ruined everything and will never be allowed to ride in the car again. Bad Linda. *Bad bad Linda!*

And that, my friends, is what writing humor is really like. Don't say you haven't been warned.

Belief Relief

It's safe to say that technology almost ruined my childhood. Or maybe saved it. The jury is still out. All I know is, I may be a gadget geek now, but when I was a child, the steady advance of technology kept my young life from being miserable.

It all started when I was eight years old, and I began to hear rumors that Santa Claus was, in fact, not a real person. My friends insisted it was their parents who bought and wrapped their gifts each year. Come to think of it, I did kinda wonder why all the tags on the gifts were in my mother's very distinct handwriting. When I confronted her about this, she answered (with a straight face, I might add), "Well, when Santa comes down the chimney with all those toys, he has a lot of work to do and not much time. I help him by filling out the tags."

Truly, my mother missed her calling as a CIA operative. She maintained her cover brilliantly. And, I believed in Santa Claus for another year.

When I was nine, my friends had lost all sympathy for me, and the teasing started. I held my ground, though. Who was I supposed to believe, my mocking friends or my dear, honest, doe-eyed mother? Yet, the suspicions grew. The doubts piled up. I might not have been very good at geometry or spatial relationships, but even I could calculate that a really fat guy wasn't going to fit down that chimney, and certainly not with a bag of toys, even if we did get too many small items like socks and new shirts for school. Besides, my mother wouldn't let some old fat dude get soot all over her nice hardwood floors.

Maybe my parents really *were* Santa Claus.

And then, that year, *The Letter* showed up.

The Letter was a feat of technology unheard of in 1970. No one could have guessed—least of all a nine-year-old girl—that, only one year after putting a man on the moon, we would have the technology to produce a letter ... from Santa Claus ... with my actual name on it ... sent through the U.S. Mail Service ... with a postmark from the North Pole!

Yes, dear reader, I was in possession of just such a letter at the tender (and highly impressionable) age of nine. In his letter, Mr. Claus (for so I would call him, to show him the respect and awe he obviously deserved) regaled me with stories of his hard work at the North Pole with the elves, mentioning how much he loved Mrs. Claus a little too often for comfort. (Frankly, it started to sound insincere after a while.)

The letter was printed on what had to be official Santa Claus/North Pole stationery: little snips of holly around the outside, and candy cane light poles in the snow, reindeer, beautiful dolls and sleds and toys.... It was enough to make a highly impressionable nine-year-old girl weep for joy. (Did I mention I was highly impressionable?)

The signature at the bottom was thrilling, yes, but the best part of the entire letter was the "Dear Linda," at the very top. *Dear Linda...*! That was *me*! Santa Claus found time in his very busy schedule to write to *me*! I looked at the envelope every few minutes, just to see my own name and address there. A personal letter from THE Santa Claus!

I took the letter—and the envelope—and showed it to as many of my friends as I could.

"See?" I said triumphantly. "Santa Claus really IS real! I have proof!"

I silenced many a skoffer and skeptic that day.

Even though I charged headlong back into childhood that day when I was nine, my mother sped up my mental and emotional development a few months later by sitting me down with her nursing school textbooks to show me where babies came from. Complete with realistic anatomical drawings. I made a pact with myself to never, *ever* get married. *Ever.*

And, I just *knew* there was something creepy about Santa talking about Mrs. Claus all the time.

That was the last year I believed in Santa Claus.

Day By Day

It's graveyard-shift time again. We're sitting at the kitchen table. We're eating dinner because it's dinner time—five o'clock P.M., to be exact—although Wayne really should be eating breakfast since he just got up fifteen minutes ago and is sitting here in his bathrobe, barefoot, eyelids still a little droopy and his "morning" medications spread out across the table next to his plate of pork chops and mashed potatoes. Pork chops and mashed potatoes are not exactly the kind of food I'd want for breakfast, if it were me getting up at 4:45 in the afternoon, but so be it. When I once asked him if he preferred eggs and sausage when he got up, he looked at me as if I'd just recited the Pledge of Allegiance in

Swahili backwards. So, even though he is working the midnight shift and sleeping during the day this entire month, he eats pork chops for breakfast, grabs lunch in the middle of the night, and stops at a local bar for hot wings and beer at seven A.M. on Wednesdays.

Doesn't really float my boat, but who am I to judge? When he's working these shifts, I end up doing laundry at midnight and washing dishes at one A.M. while he's not here so all that noise doesn't wake him up during the day.

As if the whole *what-meal-is-it?* thing isn't weird enough, I also have to get used to his odd sense of what day of the week it is. You see, his overnight shifts may start in the early evening of one day—he leaves the house by 5:30 P.M. and starts work at 6:30 and doesn't get home till 7:00 the next morning—but the work schedule officially calls that shift by the next calendar day. Therefore, it goes without saying that his Monday work shift starts at 6:30 P.M. ... on Sunday night. Well, not without saying, actually, since I just said it.

Anyway, enough with the deeply philosophical stuff.

So, as I was saying before, we're sitting at the kitchen table having our breakfast-dinner hybrid, with Wayne chewing thoughtfully on a piece of tough, overcooked pork chop smothered in barbecue sauce in order to hide the fact that it's tough and overcooked. (Sometimes that works and sometimes it doesn't. Tonight it seems to be working since he's not rolling his eyes or coughing exaggeratedly and reaching for his water glass. I thank God for small blessings.) He swallows—not choking—and frowns a bit, asking quietly, "What day is it?"

I forget that this is a trick question this month and say, "Thursday."

He nods, stuffs another forkful of pork chop in his mouth like the masochist he is, and then frowns again.

"Wait ... what day is it?"

I frown a little in return, wondering if that hearing problem he insists he does not have is getting the better of him, and say, more slowly this time, "Thurrrrrsday.... Why?"

"Oh, okay."

The mashed potatoes go down more easily than the pork chop and he's happily looking at his plate and enjoying his breakfast, one bare foot twitching on the floor and the top of his robe peeking open from across the table.

Then he stops chewing, swallows the potatoes hastily, and asks, "Wait, which Thursday?"

I assume he's asking what the date is and answer, "The third."

"Thursday, the third?"

"Yeah."

He's still frowning, this time a lot.

"What will it be tonight?"

"Still Thursday, the third."

"Oh, um..."

"Wait, do you mean after midnight? Because after midnight it'll be Friday."

"Friday," he repeats thoughtfully.

"The fourth."

"The fourth."

"Yes," I confirm, waiting to see an ecologically correct fluorescent bulb go on over his head.

"So it's really Friday then, not Thursday."

"Wait, your Friday or my Friday?" I ask, and I don't dare put any of the pork chop into my mouth right now because I find it hard to concentrate on two difficult tasks at the same time—like, chewing this pork chop and calculating days of the week with a nuke plant worker.

"My Friday, of course," he says, with more than a little bit of edge in his voice. I ignore it, since he's only been awake for fifteen minutes and his sleep was likely a bit shoddy today because there were crew workers digging up sewer lines down the street, with that annoying "beep beep beeeep" of the digger thingy backing up every two minutes all day. You try sleeping through that.

"Oh, then yes, it's Friday," I say, correcting myself, although everything in my being is screaming at me that *It's Thursday, darn it! Don't give in to his strange, warped sense of time! He's tainted this month and temporarily out of his mind!*

He nods, smiles, and picks up the last forkful of pork chop, grabbing the bottle of barbecue sauce and slathering it within an inch of its life. Apparently some mistakes are easier to cover up than others.

And now I wonder if I can dip this entire month's

calendar in barbecue sauce. Because it's going to be tough ... very, very tough.

Dinner Belle

You wouldn't know it to look at me, but I hate cooking. No, really. I detest it. I loathe it with every fiber of my being. And speaking of fiber, I hate that too.

The pressure of being the sole meal provider for others has never set well with me, and my feelings about this task don't improve with age. It's been nearly thirty years and I still hate it. The likelihood of that changing at this stage are slim to none. No, I take that back. They're just none.

I hate cooking because I am the default family cook. *How did that happen?* If I had applied for the job, I wouldn't have gotten it. And I'm pretty sure I would have remembered applying for a job like this. But somewhere along the journey, I ended up the default cook—for my entire adult life. One husband, then no husband, then husband-the-upgrade ... still I have to cook for everybody.

I think what bugs me is that, in everybody else's "real" jobs, they get feedback and bonuses and health benefits and raises. They get job incentives. They get days off ... sometimes with pay! What do I get? I get dishes left on the table, occasional "thank yous" from the kids, and gripes about emptying the dishwasher.

Let's be realistic: Why do you think wives like to be taken out to dinner? Do you think it's because the food is so much better? Usually not. It's the idea of someone else waiting on them for a change. And note: The people who wait on them get money put on the table for them! If everybody started leaving me a tip after dinner, maybe I'd be more inclined to like cooking. After all, I don't mind doing the laundry ... because I find money in everybody's pockets.

If I had to cook only for myself, I wouldn't mind it so much. What I really detest about cooking (aside from the actual act itself) is being responsible for the meals of other people from beginning to end. Cooking meals involves planning those meals, and that involves thinking about those meals—a lot. This goes back as far as grocery shopping and list-keeping. And of course, waking up each morning and fretting over what I will make for dinner that evening. It's probably my biggest work distraction of the day—worrying about exactly what I will make for dinner and making sure I have all the necessary ingredients and making sure I start far enough in advance.

By the way, the only thing worse than cooking dinner is cleaning up after it. Especially now that the portable dishwasher has decided to leak all over the kitchen floor every third time I use it, with no discernible cause.

"Honey, it looks like Lake Linda showed up again..."

My day vastly improves when I realize I've got the day's dinner planned out and all the ingredients are here and defrosting properly. My day turns into glory if I get a phone call at some point that says simply, "I won't be home for dinner, honey."

Oh, what a glorious day that is! It is doubly marvelous because not only do I not have to prepare dinner that evening, but I can just push back that day's plans for dinner to the next day, thereby taking the pressure off what to make for dinner for two days.

I cannot begin to tell you how exhilarating it feels to not have to think about dinner for days on end. To coin a phrase, it's a little taste of heaven.

Here I am now, though, looking at the clock on the wall. I see it's time for dinner again, and nobody called to cancel. A curmudgeon's work is never done.

Attack of the 50-Square-Foot Bathroom (Day 1)

We awaken one fine summer morning to the certain knowledge that, after too many years, today is the day we will begin our complete bathroom remodeling project. There is no longer any doubt about starting this project, because half the plastic tiles have fallen off the walls, because the mold on the ceiling is starting to spell out random World Book Encyclopedia entries if you look closely enough, and because the wood sub-flooring is the consistency of mulch. No, there is no doubt.

There is, however, plenty of fear. And good, old-fashioned panic. And most of it's coming from me. I'm standing in the living room, about twenty feet from the doorway of the first-floor bathroom, watching my husband, Wayne, and his brother Ed tote in sledge hammers, crow bars, and what looks suspiciously like a small nuclear device Wayne must have sneaked out of the plant under his coat.

Wayne and Ed suspect that the entire room was built around the massive cast-iron tub, and I can hear the excitement in their hushed voices as they discuss the best way to tackle the tub's demolition. Let's face it: Men like to break things with large, heavy tools, and the tub won't fit through the bathroom doorway without being smashed into smaller pieces. I personally don't have much experience smashing cast iron with a sledge hammer—I was more the bookish type in school and I don't think they even taught this in shop class. So, I position myself safely outside the bathroom and await the gleeful cry that the tub has been smashed into submission and is going to be hauled to the curb.

Let's just say it's a good thing I hadn't vowed to hold my breath until that glorious moment. Because apparently even a sledge hammer wielded by a man built like a linebacker isn't enough to coax a cast-iron tub to crumble.

Three hours, a box of Twinkies, and quite a bit of weeping later, I hear a strange sound. Besides the weeping, I mean. It sounds like something breaking. Like—dare I hope?—cast iron breaking. It is! O, the tub is rent in two! The weeping doubles down (it was Wayne weeping and Ed eating the Twinkies), and I briefly wonder if perhaps one of them has simply whacked his thumb with the sledge hammer.

But, within minutes the first section of broken tub comes rumbling out of the bathroom. Soon the old toilet that never flushed properly with just one flush is also gone, followed by the oversized porcelain sink and the rusty towel bars, as well as the few remaining green plastic tiles that have defied gravity for years and remained on the walls, taunting us ... *always taunting us.*

There is no going back now. The Great Bathroom Remodeling Project of 2009 is officially underway.

I should know better than to be excited about this. I should take up some weeping of my own, along with a little biblical gnashing of teeth. Sadly, the Twinkies are gone, along with the entire inside of the bathroom and most of my personal inner peace.

Somewhere off in the distance, I can hear a Home Depot stockholder laughing all the way to the bank....

Do-It-Yourself!

I'm a firm believer in the concept of "do-it-yourself." Now, don't think that I enjoy home improvement projects: I would just rather see *you* do it *yourself*, so *I* don't have to do it *myself*. I'm not patient about in-home projects, and I don't enjoy them in the slightest ... until the very end when the project's almost over and I can finally see why I started the darned thing in the first place. The first ninety-nine percent of the project, though, totally stinks.

Two days ago I came up to a little private campground where we have a well-equipped trailer, intending to spend three days reading, writing, and finishing a few projects. Once I got here, however, a crucial piece of software on my netbook failed on me, nixing one major project from Day One. I moved on to Project Two: making an e-book version of my first book. I was wading hip-deep in HTML code and then held my breath—and ended up with a final document with more warnings in it than the Surgeon General puts on a pack of smokes. On Day Two, there went Project Two.

Reading was the only thing left on my to-do list. I nervously looked at my e-reader sitting across the room. I had this horrible premonition that, if I turned it on, it'd either explode in a fireball, consuming the entire campground and most of the surrounding town of Slippery Rock, or it'd display all 348 books in ancient Mandarin. I sighed, strode to the sliding glass door and looked at the back deck steps, built by my dad a few years earlier and newly pressure-washed by my husband the week before. At my feet just inside the door was the can of liquid water sealant I'd bought months earlier—to protect my dad's hard work with a coat of the stuff to keep the wood from deteriorating before its time. The deck was currently as clean as when it was new, and this was my chance to do a good deed and put that sealant to work. Before I had time to talk myself out of it—which was always a distinct possibility when talking about me and house projects—I grabbed the paintbrush, the disposable plastic tray and the water seal can and headed outside.

The project seemed like a good and noble idea at the time. And, for anyone else, it probably would have been. But, for me, the tendency to overthink everything—especially when faced with a long period of time with no other mental stimuli than strong turpentine-like fumes wafting in the morning air and stray insects crawling on the deck getting in my way—ruled the day. It started with the first brush stroke: Why was I dousing the deck with a wet, watery substance just to keep out other wet, watery substances? I didn't understand the chemistry behind my activity, but philosophical questions like that merely ratcheted up the irk-factor a few notches. Sighing, I assumed the Thompson's Water Seal people knew what they were doing and bit my lip and continued.

To keep my mind off the fact that I was doing actual manual labor voluntarily—instead of reading, no less—I thought of all the stuff people don't want to see leak and began making a list of other things we could make water-tight with this marvelous, noxious stuff: water balloons, cheap swimsuits, prophylactics, babies' bottoms when they pee, my bottom when I sneeze, my eyes during a Nora Ephron movie ... the list was endless.

I decided not to crawl under the trailer to coat the underside of the deck or stairs. Only God knew what had crawled under there in the past twenty years and died, and I had no intention of lying with the squirrel carcasses or sleeping with the fishes or doing any other verb-form with dead animal skeletons. I had my pride. Plus, I'd just showered.

The most I can say about the project is that it was the easiest form of painting I'd ever done. I only had to slather copious amounts of this stuff onto the wood until all exposed surfaces (except those underneath, of course) were wet. No worries about spills or coverage or making sure the swipes all went in the same direction. Perfect project for an impatient do-it-myselfer like myself. Yet, as I moved down each step at the end of the deck, sloshing sealant like I was the Pope and it was holy water over the crowd off that big balcony of his, I had to crouch a little lower, feeling my knees lock up and knowing I was aging at least five years per step. I was glad the deck had only four steps, even if they were suddenly a lot wider than they had a right to be.

Halfway into the project, I caught out of the corner of my eye some movement on the deck. A creepy, long-legged, red and black spider was making its way across a portion of the deck I had just splashed, and it wasn't moving all that gracefully. I had trouble counting its legs as it hobbled across the wet wood, but last time I was in biology class, I remembered learning that arachnids had eight legs. This poor schmoe was limping along with a few fewer than eight. Even I, an English major, could count high enough to see that. It had a long way to go to get off the deck to wherever it was headed, and I seriously doubted it would live to see the end of its journey. It was probably screaming little high-pitched spidey-screams that were out of my range of hearing as it shuffled.

So now, in the middle of what should have been a simple, mindless task (and do-it-myself good deed) came a moral dilemma worthy of PETA. For a few minutes I continued swabbing the deck and tried to ignore the pathetic, ugly, icky spider creeping haphazardly across the deck like a drunken sailor. Should I leave it alone, letting it find its way in the world, hoping naively that it would somehow live out the day missing at least two legs and with its remaining five or six coated with Thompson's Water Seal? Or, horror of emotional horrors, should I put it out of its misery with the wooden end of the paintbrush? As if it knew I was mulling over its fate, it began crawling a little faster away from me and toward the corner of the deck. Not a lot faster. Just a little. I mean, it was missing two or three legs, after all. Just when I was beginning to worry that I'd never come to a firm ethical decision, I remembered an important fact: I hate spiders.

Problem solved. And, best of all, I did it myself.

Hair Today, Hair Tomorrow

I'm back to getting my hair cut. Well, it's not that I was ever *not* getting my hair cut, even if only by myself using a mirror, some plastic Crayola scissors, and a lot of prayer. But, for many of my adult years, I wore my hair long ... and straight ... and boring ... and cheap. This was perhaps the only advantage to being a poor woman most of my adult life, rather than a poor man: I could get by without having to pay someone to cut my hair as long as I wore it long and straight and boring. Since that also described most of my existence, why not have hair to match?

But, a few years ago, as I continued to age against my will, I realized that, unless I started braiding my hair, wearing Laura Ashley dresses and using terms like "sister wives," it was time for me to have a hairstyle instead of just hair. It took almost a year to get used to the idea of paying for a haircut every six to eight weeks, so I adapted by using coupons and going to one of several large "chain" styling salons near my house. Yes, I know what you're thinking: How classy.

You know the kind of place I mean: It's nestled just inside my local Walmart next to the generic eye doctor, the customer service department, the genderless "family" bathroom, and the greeter with the blue smock who annoys the crap out of me by cheerily starting a conversation about the routinely poor local weather while I'm desperately trying to unhook a single shopping cart from the long line of carts to which it has apparently been welded fast. Anyway, for under twenty bucks I can get in and out of one of these places looking decent enough to be seen in public, which is pretty much the main goal of ever getting one's hair cut. If I suffered from agoraphobia and never left the house, I could save a ton of money on haircuts. And clean clothing. And bathing. And ... I'd better quit before I give myself any more bad ideas.

There are down sides to saving money on haircuts the way I do. The most glaring is those magazines. When I first worked up the nerve to get my long, straight, boring hair cut off, I sat in the waiting area, listening to the Walmart greeter a few feet away as he verbally frisked everyone on their way into the store complex. I waded through one hairstyle magazine after another, hoping to find one with a picture somewhat close to the concept I had in my head, so we could get it ONTO my head correctly. But, of course, none of the women looked anything like me. They were all moody, pencil-thin models with sleek, ridiculous hairstyles that looked more like avant-garde architecture on display in the Museum of Modern Art. Did any of these women think they could go out in a stiff breeze with hair like that? Actually, most of them looked like they'd just come in from being out in a stiff breeze and couldn't find a hairbrush.

I gave up on visual aids after combing through even the men's magazines, figuring I wouldn't look all that great in a buzz cut anyway and I'd likely send a lot of the wrong signals besides. I was going to have to use my preferred medium of communication—words—to describe to the stylist what I envisioned. I felt sorry for her. She had no idea I was just about to ruin her day. I had confidence in her abilities, though, since her own hair looked so disastrously bad. That could only mean that one of the *other* stylists in the shop sucked. I cut down the odds of my own haircut sucking by at least one stylist.

Another down side to cheap haircuts is that, while I am waiting my turn, all the stylists seem to be working on people they know. They all banter with their customers as they chop and snip and tweak and tease, and everybody seems to be sharing inside jokes. Jokes I don't get. Jokes I'm not privy to. And they are all younger than I am. Much younger. Like, I-don't-have-to-color-my-hair-yet younger.

"So," the stylist asks during that first visit, as if we are already in the middle of a conversation we haven't started yet, "what kind of style are you looking for?"

I want to say, "The perfect kind, you idiot," but I restrain myself. "Shoulder-length or shorter," I say. "Layered."

"Layered, or feathered?" she asks.

It hasn't occurred to me until this moment that there is a difference. I try not to sound confused but know I've never been that great an actress.

"Feathered. Yes, feathered. I want to say kind of like a shag, but ..."

"Well, that would be layered then," she corrects. Now I'm lost and I fear if I say much more, I'll end up looking like my sixth grade school photo, and I'm not sure I can get a hold of a granny-square crocheted vest in earth tones to complete the look properly.

"No, feathered. I meant feathered."

"You mean, like from the seventies?"

I bite my lip. One false nod and I won't be able to leave the house for months.

"Bangs?" she asks.

Who knew getting my hair cut would be a game of Twenty Questions? Hard questions.

"Well, I have this short forehead. See?" I pull back my long locks to expose my teeny tiny forehead. I know there are worse fates than a short forehead—after all, my husband's forehead seems to be expanding every year along with his waistline and I don't think he's all that thrilled about either one—but in my case, it might mean bangs are a bad idea.

The stylist frowns and tsk-tsks at me, waving a pair of scissors around my face in the most unseemly fashion. I hope she doesn't need glasses—because she isn't wearing any and my life is flashing before my eyes faster than those scissors.

"Yes, we'll feather this all back then," she agrees, and she starts cutting. Now, since that first haircut, I've gotten used to the sound of the first snip of the scissors, but that day, with hair cascading halfway down my back, I knew how Samson must have felt. And in my experience, empathy with biblical characters never ends well.

I let her continue cutting, and I avoid looking in the huge wall mirror by glancing to the left, where I see a woman in the waiting area who will be sitting in this chair after me. According to her roots, she has long, straight thinning gray hair, but she colors it an unnaturally dark black. She has obviously gone months since her last coloring and she has roots that look like something Moses has already parted to let the entire Hebrew nation through. I pray silently that she is here for a professional coloring to cover up that odd skunk stripe running down the middle of her head.

And, I sigh loudly and relax about my own haircut, knowing even a shag could work if I walk with enough confidence while searching the thrift store for a crocheted poncho and a pair of hip-hugger bell-bottoms.

You're Getting Sleeeeeeepy ...

Now that I freelance completely and don't have to commute to a daily job (thanks to my hard-working, nuclear-power-plant-employed engineer-husband), I find that I've turned into a sort of sleep-chameleon, adapting to his ever-changing schedule. He does what's called "shift work," meaning that he'll work a semi-normal day shift for a few weeks and then has to work a middle shift for a week, and then an overnight shift for another week.

I don't know how he does it, but he seems to adapt easily, a quality I wish I possessed in greater amounts. He's very laid back about most things, including whether he gets enough sleep and when that sleep happens. How he can fall into a deep sleep in our sun-laden bedroom during the day while construction workers, loud children, and garbage trucks are all zipping around outside is beyond me. Yet another reason I adore the guy: He rolls with the punches.

And me? By the end of his overnight shift week, I'm staying up till four in the morning myself, tweaking something on my computer till it bleeds while watching a marathon of *Storage Wars* on A&E in the background, volume up to ear-splitting decibels just because nobody's home and I can.

The guinea pigs in my office haven't complained yet. Then again, I bribe them with celery and carrots and they doesn't speak good English, so perhaps they're royally peeved at me and I just can't tell with those blank stares of theirs.

At any rate, last night was one of those nights. I revamped my entire Web site and blog all day and long into the night, gulping down glass after glass of sugar-free lemonade and yelling at the television for Darrell to just buy the stupid storage locker and take his chances already.

It was glorious fun for a night owl, and I love that I get a week like this every month or so, when I can indulge my inner college student. I'll be sad to see it go after tonight, with hubby back on early-morning duty on Saturday. I'll get up, bleary-eyed, and make him breakfast before he leaves, with the sky still dark outside, but then I'll head straight back to bed for a few hours, zonking into oblivion until the sun comes up and the sleep hours add up to something a lot closer to eight than he usually gets.

Some of us are just more adaptable than others.

Secret Love Affairs with Broccoli Cheddar Soup

I'm sitting at my local Panera Bread, slurping some hot broccoli cheddar soup, sipping a Diet Pepsi and wondering whether product placement in these essays will get me some free stuff. Probably not. Probably somebody in charge has to actually *read* this before I'd see a gift card or a truckload of free broccoli cheddar soup for a year. Besides, where would I put it? I mean, I can eat the stuff every single day, but even doing the math, it'd take at least a month to get through a truckload of soup. A very, very pleasant month....

I seem to do my most efficient writing outside my home, and I know I'm not the only writer who has experienced this strange phenomenon. I sometimes wonder why I tell people that I work from home, since that's the last place I get any actual work done. Unless you count laundry and housecleaning, which I don't. I try never to think about laundry or housecleaning if I can help it. I'm proud to say it usually works. If you don't believe me, you should see the inside of my house. Come to think of it, no, you shouldn't.

But I digress.

I've written in more than a dozen different Panera locations across the country, as well as in most of my local libraries—in several adjacent counties, no less—and in every Starbucks within a twenty-mile radius. The local McDonald's will work in a pinch, especially if it has free WiFi.

Over the past few years, I've developed a laundry list (yes, I know, a laundry list) of things I look for in a writing-home-away-from-home. These items rearrange themselves in different orders of importance depending on my mood, but the list itself remains fairly static.

First, the place has to have free WiFi. I like to sit down, fire up the netbook, and immediately announce on Facebook that I've arrived and am writing up a storm while enjoying my favorite [coffee, soup, soda, greasy hamburger] ... (but not all of them at the same time). Then, while I'm struggling to pull ten or twelve words out of my brain in some sort of logical order, I have a virtual cheering section of people who "like" my status or who keep up with my otherwise boring escapades out in the real world.

I particularly appreciate that so many of my online friends have no real lives or hobbies of their own and get excited to hear I've just refilled my Diet Pepsi and decided not to eat the hunk of bread. I'd beg them all to get a life, but then I wouldn't have my cheering section and I'd end up having to actually write while I'm here.

Also, the free WiFi has to come without a boatload of weird hoops to jump through. In most places now, they no longer make me change my browser settings under some Advanced tab where I have to manually input DNS server numbers and differentiate between WPA and WEP password variations and calculate Pi to the hundredth digit and submit my Social Security number and SAT scores to a panel of experts who'll get back to me next Tuesday with a string of letters and numbers to input on a strange Web page that looks suspiciously like a scam to get me to buy gold coins to hedge against the coming societal meltdown.

By the time I figured out how to get online in those days, I had to leave.

If I'm at an eatery and not in a library, I feel better if they have coffee. Good coffee. I'm not sure how I define "good coffee," but I know it when I smell it. And when I pay for it.

I'll tolerate writing in a Starbucks but I try not to get their humongous cups of coffee (whatever their vaguely Italian-sounding word is for "gargantuan cup") because it always tastes as if the coffee beans were not only roasted but tortured, maimed, and run through a nuclear reactor before being brewed.

And don't get me started on their whole "Tall" and "Grande" and "Venti" business. I'm five-foot-two and I'd be the last person to call myself "tall"—and I'm a heck of a lot taller than that cup. They're not fooling anybody. Plus, I just went to their Web site to jog my memory since I couldn't remember the word "Venti," and it says in big, bold lettering, "Handcrafted beverages."

Excuse me? Since when is a cup of coffee "handcrafted"? Now I'm picturing someone sitting in the corner crocheting a coffee cup for me using bamboo hooks. That's probably not what they mean by "handcrafted," but it would sure explain their prices. Call me cheap, but I prefer coffee that I don't have to take out a second mortgage to pay for.

I also prefer my coffee a little smoother than the fare at Starbucks. Specifically, I prefer the coffee at my locally owned coffee shop, Cafe Kolache. It's coffee that tastes smooth but doesn't have to be handpicked by former fourth-world ex-slaves whose daughters were sold into the sex trade. And I'm pretty sure no puppies or kittens were harmed in the making of their coffee either. So, it's a win-win for everybody.

Plus, Starbucks coffee is so hot it should come with a nuclear exposure micro-sievert warning on the side of those double-walled, corrugated-sleeved cups. I suppose they make their coffee so scalding hot because every Starbucks I've ever been in has been freezing cold, winter or summer. They have to warm you up somehow. I usually just bring a parka, some mittens, and earmuffs any time I go there to write. But I never get very much work done. You try typing with mittens on.

Before I completely ruin my chances of getting free product placement stuff from Starbucks, let me continue. The one really great thing about Starbucks—which is also true of the Paneras and my beloved Cafe Kolache—is that they don't seem to mind if you buy a single cup of coffee, monopolize a table, plug in a laptop, use their WiFi, and then conduct a small business in the corner for the next few hours. It's become so commonplace that I'm thinking of having their address put on my next order of business cards.

I see by the clock in my netbook's computer tray (and the balance on my Panera gift card) that it's time to head home. I'll have to update my Facebook status first so that my fan club can wish me well, express their envy at my exotic, continental lifestyle, and ask me for more cows and chickens on Farmville.

Because, for a writer, it's all about priorities.

Stranger Danger

It's natural for adults to look back on their childhoods and remember only the good parts—especially middle-aged adults with limited brain space left after raising multiple children through the teen years. You know what I'm talking about ... or maybe you don't because of that limited brain space thing. We tend to idealize our pasts and call those times the "golden years" or the "good ol' days" or something else equally ridiculous and untrue. We're probably trying to impress our kids, or maybe just to make them feel envious of us. You know, because they're already better off than we were at their age, and in reality we're the envious ones because we would have asked Santa for an iPod for Christmas if the thing had been invented back in 1975.

Strangely, the same parents who romanticize their childhoods to impress their children will malign those same childhoods in the next breath ... to impress the same children. Even stranger, it often works. This goes way beyond the stereotypical line of "When I was your age, I had to walk to school in the snow uphill ... both ways."

And, I admit, I've succumbed to the technique with my own kids. They've heard the horror stories of just how unsafe and dangerous it was to be a child growing up in the sixties and seventies. I suppose they won't fully appreciate just how naively dangerous our childhoods were, but I've had a few isolated opportunities to show my kids what we were up against back then.

One such opportunity came when I dug out my old, yellow Easy Bake Oven from the office closet so my daughter and I could make tiny little useless cakes. I'd kept it all these years, dragged it from apartment to apartment to house every time we moved, and there wasn't any reason it shouldn't still work. I found a 100-watt incandescent light bulb in the linen closet and we were off!

As we peeked in the little slot at the end of the oven, watching the teeny little chocolate cake rise, I realized nobody in Research and Development these days would have gotten away with designing a kids' toy that uses the raw heat from a 100-watt bulb to cook things.

The thing has a picture on the box of a very young girl with her hands on the oven at both ends, dangerously close to that hot end where the bulb is doing its glorious, hazardous magic. And yet, every girl I knew had one of these things.

Nowadays, it'd take a little cake about three days to bake under one of those newfangled curly fluorescent light bulbs. Hardly worth it, really, when you could bake an entire full-sized cake on the front sidewalk in August. And of course, the new Easy Bake Ovens look like little microwaves. Please. Spare me.

I had two toys that used sharp objects as essential parts of the toy. One was the old Mr. Potato Head, which had its body parts made of pointy plastic that they suggested you stick into a real raw potato. Which I did. Which my mother didn't appreciate on nights she was hoping to use those potatoes for dinner. Which got me into a lot of trouble. But honestly, the real potatoes, with their different shapes, were so much more fun than using the boring plastic "potato" that came in the box.

Perhaps the worst toy I owned, in terms of personal peril, was my Spirograph. It was also my personal favorite. The gist of this genius invention was to use some of Mom's straight pins to anchor a piece of paper and these little plastic wheels and cogs onto a piece of corrugated cardboard. Then, I stuck the point of a colored pen into a tiny hole in one of the cogs or wheels (I get them confused—remember, I was an English major) and whisked it around and around inside the outer wheel, creating these cool round or oval shapes on the paper.

If I changed one of the cogs (or wheels—don't get technical on me now) and the color of the pen, going back over the same design, I could create a cool, psychedelic design to hang on the bulletin board in my room (you know, the one with the flower-power design painted right on the cork).

Now, assuming I didn't pull too hard on the pen and let centrifugal force (or is it centripetal force? English major! *English major!*) yank the pins out of the cardboard (a big assumption), it was a very cool toy that created some amazing designs.

But, even assuming I didn't lance myself with a straight pin or bend them in half, rendering them useless to my mother, the biggest issue I had with the Spirograph is that it should have come with a warning for us klutzy people. I can't begin to relate the anguish in my teen heart after I'd spent hours (okay, minutes) changing pens and cogs and wheels and restraightening pins ... only to have my uncoordinated hand slip on the last color, the pen sliding up and out of the tiny little plastic hole and scratching a long haphazard green line right across the finished design.

O no! O, Spirograph! *O, the humanity!*

Come to think of it, I hated that thing.

In comparison to the evil Spirograph, the rest of my toys were, well, child's play. Barbie dolls came with tiny shoes that smaller children could easily swallow. That's probably the real reason they put holes in the bottoms of all her shoes—not so that you could put her on one of those stands. It was so toddlers could still get air into their passageways if (when) they swallowed the bits of plastic thinking they were deformed Skittles.

The prize for most obvious tiny bits of plastic, though, has to go to the Lite Brite. The thing came with about twenty-seven thousand little bits of colored plastic—luring and coaxing little children for miles around to come and taste the yummy little candies that came with their older sister's Big Girl Toy. I have a brother who is two years younger than I am. He got into more trouble in a week than I could even conjure up in a year—so this explains why my mother waited till I was twenty-five before I got my first Lite Brite. By then I had two toddler sons of my own. Good going, Grandma.

Since I still have my Easy Bake Oven, I must still have that Lite Brite. It's probably somewhere buried in that same closet, next to the Easy Bake Oven and the Rock 'Em Sock 'Em Robots and the metal Tonka truck Jeep with the windshield that folded down and pinched my fingers.

Those were indeed the good ol' days, as long as you had good medical coverage.

Driving Me Crazy, the Sequel

I've made the grave error of telling my parents I'll go with them to an outdoor flea market in neighboring Ohio. Don't get me wrong: I'm glad my parents are neat and tidy and organized and have a routine. But, trying to shoehorn myself into that routine always turns into a low-level feeling of strangulation. I love going to the flea market, but part of the fun is a feeling of spontaneity and adventure. Going with my parents is like going on a field trip in kindergarten. All that's missing is wearing a kid-leash, holding hands using the buddy system, and a playground whistle. I mean, my mom tried to make me do all that the first time we went, but I put my foot down and said no. I drew the line at the harness, but I had to promise I wouldn't cross the street without looking both ways first.

Even though Roger's Flea Market is open every Friday till about 10:00 P.M., my parents go early in the morning, meaning I have to be at their house by about 9:30 A.M. Not dreadfully early to most people, but I work from home now, so 9:30 is an ungodly hour to be up, dressed, fed, and driving a car voluntarily ... especially to go somewhere, walk around in mud, and haggle with people speaking Chinese over the inflated $1 price of twenty-five generic batteries or a plastic back scratcher. I do my best haggling in late afternoon, at the earliest.

But, this is their outing and I'm outnumbered already, so I comply and show up in their driveway at 9:32, just as my mother is calling my cell phone to ask me where I am. I make a mental note to protect myself for the future by turning all their clocks back fifteen minutes while they're in the bathroom, but of course, they're already done getting ready and my plan is foiled.

I grab my keys, my purse, and my cell phone and get out of my car, locking the door. My dad is in the driveway preparing their car for the trip. This means putting one of the back seats down so that their two-wheeled folded shopping cart can fit into the back alongside me. He has an old blanket tucked under the cart, and another one on top of the cart.

At first I think it's to keep the cart warm, which doesn't make sense because it's August, but then I realize he's done this to make sure none of the cart's spiky, pointy metal parts harm me or the car if it jostles around during the trip. I fight the urge to suggest he wrap the whole thing in bubble wrap next time, because I don't want to give him any ideas. The man has no sense of humor sometimes, and I look terrible in bubble wrap. And don't ask me how I know that. My husband thought it was a good idea at the time.

Meanwhile, Dad's busy loading things into the hatch of their PT Cruiser: a cooler, more blankets, three bottles of water, a sunhat, the liner for the two-wheeled cart, a fanny pack, and about 437 elastic bungee cords in 13 different sizes.

I don't know what it is about men and those bungee cords, but every guy I know keeps a few dozen of them in his trunk. I think it's why my dad and my husband get along so well: They're constantly admiring each other's bungee cord collection.

But I digress. The trunk now looks as if we are going on safari instead of just to Ohio. Which, by the way, is about fifteen miles away.

Once my dad gets the car packed up, we all pile in. I am a good daughter and sit in the back seat with the two-wheeled cart, right behind my dad, who keeps asking me if I have enough leg room. It's a midsized car, I'm 5'2" and he's about 5'7", so yes, I have plenty of leg room. I could hold a clog dance tournament in front of my knees with all the leg room I have. I'd have to actually have adult-sized legs for the leg room to even start being a problem, and I don't. So, we're fine.

"You *sure* you got enough leg room back there?"

"Yup, Dad, I'm fine."

He adjusts his seat forward a few more inches.

"No, really, I'm fine. You don't have to move the seat. I have at least six inches of room in front of my knees already."

"Okay," he says and moves the seat forward another three or four inches.

My mom is busy in the front passenger seat readjusting her seat belt and the four air vents in front of her.

"You getting enough air back there?" she asks over her left shoulder, turning her head just enough to indicate she is talking to me and not my dad, but not actually turning enough to make eye contact with me. It looks as if she is talking to the rearview mirror, which, I'm sure, is getting enough air.

Besides, it's not like we're sitting in a vacuum. I'm getting air, for crying out loud. If she sees me gasping and turning blue and fainting in the back seat, then maybe I'm not getting enough air.

"It's fine, Mom. Whatever works for you."

She chills easily. It's August. But, she chills easily.

"Because I can always turn up the air conditioning."

"No, that's fine. I can always put the window down if I need to."

She gasps. "Not if I have the air conditioning on!" This seems to be a thing with both her and my dad, as if the air conditioning system will implode if someone opens a window while it's running. It's the same rule as the refrigerator: Never stand with the door open because you'll let the cold out. Apparently my mother keeps an inventory list of all the items in her fridge on the door with a bunch of those fridge magnets so she never has to open the door to see what's in there.

"Okay, okay, I won't put the window down. But, I'm fine," I assure her. She doesn't sound assured. She's clicking her tongue and fussing with the four air vents. Neither my dad or I mind because this means she's not paying as much attention to his driving.

I, on the other hand, am doing nothing *but* paying attention to my dad's driving. One thing I'd forgotten about driving in a car with my parents during all those years we lived hundreds or even thousands of miles apart is that it feels as if my dad is tapping out the rhythm of some Johnny Cash song in his head with his foot on the brake. We'll be driving along at a decent clip and then *BAM!* the brakes get a tap and the seat belts pull up short and we all get the wind knocked out of us. *That's* when I'm not getting enough air.

My dad also has this irrational love of driving on winding back roads (he calls them "scenic"), and so we are now meandering around somewhere in the limbo between Pennsylvania and Ohio, careening around bends and corners at twice the local speed limit, my dad's foot brushing the brake enough for me to lurch forward and feel my uvula clamp up in the back of my throat. I'm trying to figure out which Johnny Cash song this rhythm goes with, if only to keep my mind off the fact that I'm prone to motion sickness, the windows are all closed, and my mother, who chills easily, is in control of the air conditioning in the front seat, meaning it's probably not on at all.

I would like to find the Dramamine in my purse, even if it's long past its expiration date because I only need it when I'm in their car, but my purse is now wedged under the two-wheeled cart and its blanket alongside me. If we careen a little to the right, I might be able to grab it and yank it free, but the mere act of leaning any more in that direction makes me throw up a little bit in my mouth. And, the bottles of water I'd like to use to wash the Dramamine down are in the cooler back in the hatch with the rest of the safari gear.

By the time we get to the flea market, turn the last corner, and slow down enough to find the perfect parking spot on the grassy field, I regret everything I've eaten in the past two days and I think I've become permanently cross-eyed from trying to find a way to look out the window without getting more nauseous.

I close my eyes and try not to listen as they start the long "discussion" of where to park.

"That's not a spot, John. There's a pole in the middle of it."

"I know. I wasn't going to park there. I see a spot further down."

"At the end? We'll have to walk all the way back."

"Well, it looks like it's the best we can find today."

"It's not my fault your daughter was late this morning."

I was *two minutes* late. Dad was still packing the car anyway. And I love how she says "your daughter" whenever I do something wrong. If I ever win the Nobel Prize for Literature, you can bet I'll be ***her*** daughter that day.

"***You*** wanna drive on the trip home? Because that can be arranged."

I start kicking the back of his seat. The last thing we want is for my mother to drive home, in control of everything on the dashboard.

"No, John, just park anywhere. I don't care."

Nobody's buying that "I don't care" business. If he parks in the wrong spot, he'll never hear the end of it.

Meanwhile, I'm in the back seat trying to get enough intestinal equilibrium to walk around in ninety-degree scorching heat at the outdoor flea market while still feeling seasick from the car ride up here. As soon as the car is parked—only about a half-mile from the closest vendors, with nary a tree in sight, I might add—I push the door open and collapse out onto the grass, gasping for breath and feeling my head spin with both motion sickness and several unresolved childhood issues.

All I can think of now is that I'd better find a damned nice plastic back scratcher for a dollar. Otherwise, this trip might not be worth it.

Fear This! (and this ... and this!)

It's therapeutic for me to list things that I'm afraid of. Not necessarily for you, but certainly for me. Writing this whole book is a kind of therapy, really. Bear with me while I unleash some of my less violent psychoses on you.

Below you'll find only a partial list of things that scare me, since it would take a book closer to the size of an encyclopedia to cover everything I'm afraid of. But this list gets us started. Are you taking notes? This will be on the quiz.

* **Flying.**
* *No, wait. Not flying. Crashing. Let's start this again.*
* **Crashing.**

* **Rats.**

* **Bats.**

* *Wait, on that previous one, you know I meant the mammal bats, right? Not baseball bats. Because baseball bats aren't really anything to be afraid of – unless Tony Soprano is coming at you with one. Oh rats, let's get the rhythm back here.*

* **Crashing.**

* **Rats.**

* **Bats.**

* **Cats.** No, wait, that's my husband. He's afraid of almost any animal in the house that doesn't live in an aquarium or some sort of airtight enclosure. Which includes pretty much any sentient being besides me and him ... and several of our children. (And so much of that hinges on one's definition of "sentient.")

* **Lightning.** No, wait, wait, that was when I was a kid. Back then I read that, during a lightning storm, a person is ninety-seven percent safe in a house – and one-hundred percent safe in a car. So, any time a thunderstorm started, that three percent difference had me looking longingly at my mom's Ford Pinto in our driveway. It looked so very ... *safe*. Well, that is, until 1978, when they were all recalled because they would explode if someone hit them from behind.

* **Bees** flying into my open soda can.

* Come to think of it, ***anything*** flying into my open soda can. Because, certainly if a rabid pterodactyl flew into it, I'd be afraid of that too.

* **Running out of coffee**. Okay, I realize that's not on par with finding a rabid pterodactyl in my can of

Sierra Mist, but it's scary. Trust me. Nobody wants to see me devoid of all traces of caffeine.

* **Doughnuts.** In my house. Unsupervised.

* **My husband** getting that seductive, coy look in his eye—the one that says, "I think I'll start remodeling the den."

The Grass Is Always Longer …

I'm going to die out here in this God-forsaken jungle. That's all I can think of—a sudden, sharp panic setting into my brain and a certain fear gripping my soul. I think of my family—husband, children, my parents—and wish I had told them one last time that I love them or otherwise had some words of wisdom to leave with them. I fret that the last thing I said to Wayne was, "Why are you the only man on earth who not only puts the toilet seat down but also puts the lid down? It's not like we have dogs or anything!" Not a good way to be remembered.

The kids will probably remember me as the mom who had trouble keeping up with what foods they liked, continuing to serve them pepperoni casserole well into their twenties because "it's your favorite," when it probably stopped being their favorite sometime in the 1990s, not long after Barney the dinosaur stopped being their favorite. Wait, he was never their favorite, and I remember at the time thanking God for small mercies. Anyway, at least they'll have fond memories of borrowing my Pearl Jam albums....

I'm yanked out of my wistful deathbed reverie by the sound of something stalking me from the bushes off to my right. At dusk like this, it could be almost anything coming after me, ready to pounce and claw at my neck and face, sucking the life blood out of me until I die gasping for breath, clutching at the ground, gathering the rich soil in my free hand, smelling its earthiness and knowing any moment I'll be returning to it, from whence I came.

"Linda, the phone's for you!"

I snap back to reality, look around me here on the patio, and see that the waist-high grass in our back yard might be overrun with chipmunks and some earthworms, but probably little else. Or so Wayne tells me. Tonight, I'm not buying it.

"Okay, I'll be right in!" I call from the padded wrought-iron lounge chair, hidden behind the overgrown wheat field that used to be our yard.

How did we let it get this bad? I wonder, when I'm finished on the phone and come back outside to continue working at the patio table, a tall glass of sugar-free lemonade by my side as my lone companion in this sea of greenery gone wild. Nobody else in this entire zip code has waited until mid-May to mow their back yards. Just us. And we're new here, so I know we're not making a good first impression on the neighbors. The pile of rubble and debris under the second-floor bathroom window doesn't help either, but it can't be helped because it's taking us a ridiculous amount of time to get the bathroom remodeled before we can live here 24/7 instead of having to drive back to the old house to take a shower every day. I keep reminding myself that all of this seemed like a good idea at the time, but I bet Francesco Schettino said the same thing to himself. No consolation there, really.

I'd rather be sitting up on the back porch than on this open brick patio, shielded by the porch roof from the sun and the bombardment of random bird poop, but the massive back porch is engulfed by the old bathroom fixtures and some of the new ones: an old toilet, two old sinks, the new/old claw foot tub (new to us, old to the rest of the world)... plus a few trees' worth of lumber and plywood sitting haphazardly on various pairs of sawhorses. Not to mention the six-foot wall mirror, which miraculously hasn't broken despite having leaned up against the porch railing for the past four months. A few times I thought I might pretend the rusted old toilet was a quirky Adirondack chair or that the sinks were little concave end tables on which to rest my lemonade, but somehow that just didn't work out the way I'd envisioned it. I can only hope none of my neighbors were watching through their windows with a camera. That's not really the way I'd want to see myself on YouTube for the first time.

Birds started nesting in the clawfoot tub until I shooed them away. They just set up housekeeping in the porch rafters instead. Needless to say, *their* move didn't take five months. Needless to say, *they* didn't decide to remodel their only full bathroom before moving into the rafters. No… that was the brilliant idea of the evolutionarily superior human beings.

Wait … What was that sound? I thought I heard something scraping, crawling through the grass. Are those evil eyes I see peering at me from between the dandelion fronds, fronds so large they look almost prehistoric? Is that a raptor cooing at me from behind the caradonna plant? I think the mourning dove on the overhead wire has her eye on me and will swoop down to either slice open my jugular vein or just steal a sip of the lemonade when I'm not looking. She's probably in cahoots with the pterodactyl I'm positive is hovering just over my right shoulder in the Japanese maple tree.

Oh, dear Lord, protect me! I'm sure I just felt something slither under the patio table and over my feet while I was busy looking over my other shoulder to see if that squirrel was plotting his revenge in the rhododendron. I knew I should have found time to trim that thing back because now he probably has an entire army of angry, vengeful squirrels back there, every one of them rabidly upset with me because I switched from expensive pecans to cheap party peanuts and stale cornbread whenever I tried to make friends with them by tossing treats out into the back yard. And maybe I shouldn't use the word "rabid" when talking about wild rodents.

Or maybe they're upset because the grass is so tall that they can't even tell if there *are* treats in the back yard anymore. I know I can't tell. We'll probably have pecan bushes and peanut trees growing there next spring, or whatever those things grow from. Heck, I can't even tell where the fence starts or ends because the grass looks more like I'm trying to take up corn farming and fool everybody.

I think there was a trampoline back in the left corner of the yard, but my memory is a little foggy on that point. If I ever venture out into the yard (wearing a pair of safety goggles, a gas mask, and some hip-high fishing waders, just to be safe), and I hit a spot where I bounce into the air five feet and whack my head on the garage gutter, that's probably where the trampoline is.

And Murray, my beloved guinea pig, who passed away two months ago, is going to come back to haunt me from somewhere beyond the Rainbow Bridge. And I'll deserve it too. I buried him one rainy day in the farthest corner of the yard, marking the spot with several patio stones, intending to paint something poignant on one of them someday soon. But that day never came, and now I'll be lucky if I ever see that corner of the yard again without a cached Google Maps overhead view. If we ever cut this grass and I can safely venture back there again, I'll probably find his little piggy paw sticking up out of the ground, digits curled in a little piggy fist, cursing me from beyond the grave for not tending to his resting place properly. The ghost of Murray, more revenge from Mother Nature.

Must every single creature on God's earth mock me while I sit here? When I had hoped to sit peacefully in the back yard, among nature and fresh air, like normal people do, I had no idea just how frightening the experience would be, all because we left the gasoline in our lawn mower last autumn and now the thing is clogged up worse than me when I eat way too much cheese. And Wayne's stubbornly tried to cut the front yard with that lawn mower three times now, each time more frustrating than the last. The first time, he only got the front yard 75 percent finished before the machine either ran out of gas (again) or just went on strike in protest of unfair working conditions.

What an embarrassment it was to live on the main drag running through town, and to have the only front lawn wearing a green Mohawk down the middle. It wasn't a good time to introduce ourselves to the neighbors *that* week either. And now I'm really afraid to introduce ourselves because if they come over here, the rest of their families may never see them again. We've begun asking our friends or guests to be sure they've made out their wills before we'll allow them to set foot on our property. We can at least be that neighborly, can't we?

As I sit here musing over how to get back into the good graces of the folks around us—not that we were ever *in* their good graces to begin with—I know I've heard something stirring in the pile of old wood, broken tiles, and fiberglass shower walls strewn about the yard just off the back porch, where it all landed after being hoisted out the upstairs bathroom window during the early demolition phase. That pile's seen the frigid snows of winter, the wet thaw of early spring, and now the overgrown jungle of summer, and I'm fairly certain it's now home to several moles (or shrews or whatever those fast black frantic animals are that army-crawl from the pile of bricks like the devil's chasing them), a grossly inbred family of chipmunks, and other disease-ridden rodentia too numerous to keep track of or think about for very long without feeling a little twitchy.

And just now, the bald, mangy squirrel who's the most frightened of me (which is ironic since she's the one who's got folds of pink, scabby skin and a tail with only half its fur on it—talk about scary, girlfriend! See a vet, would you?) is sitting in the magnolia tree, breathing strangely, darting her eyes around as if she knows something I don't, and refusing to come down to get the lousy party peanuts I'm trying to toss onto the sidewalk where she can see them. She won't come down, even when I switch to the pecans, and just sits in the crook of a branch just above eye level with me, staring at me as if I'm crazy to think she'll set foot on the ground here in this yard without a chaperone until we do something about the weeds and grass.

As I give up on coaxing the squirrel from her safety in the tree, Wayne comes out of the house and heads for his truck, not daring to veer from the sidewalk or driveway for fear of disappearing without a trace and ending up on the side of a milk carton next month.

"Where are you going?" I ask, upset that he's willing to leave me here all alone, unprotected in this jungle after the sun sets. I can hear the fear in my own voice, smell the sweat that's broken out on me as I watch him get into the truck and roll down the window. He backs the truck up and turns toward me.

"I'm going to Home Depot. They're having a sale on sickles."

I think I'm relieved.

Go, my beloved husband – go with God's blessing ... and mine.

Baldy the Squirrel

I've got a pet squirrel. Well, not exactly a pet, though I like to think that he belongs to me. He lives somewhere in the general vicinity of our house and annoys me several times a day with his bold and insistent begging for food. With a description like that, he's either a pet or one of my kids.

Although our new house is right on the main drag of our little borough, the back yard is large and fenced well enough to give all manner of wild creatures a false sense of security. We're not completely moved in yet, but I've already overfed cardinals, robins, chickadees, blue jays, finches, sparrows, mourning doves, a short-tailed shrew, a nest of baby bunnies, one highstrung chipmunk and two fox squirrels.

It started innocently enough when I saw an old bird feeder that the previous owners had left hanging from a low branch of the magnolia tree right outside our back door. I bought some bird seed for the feeder, loaded it up, and stood stunned as, within minutes, the thing had attracted so many birds that it would have made Alfred Hitchcock nervous. It looked like the freebie food sample line at Sam's Club on a weekend.

I learned quickly that a bird feeder attracts more than just birds. A squirrel started hanging out just under the feeder, an area I dubbed the Foraging Frenzy. At first I worried that he was rabid or diseased because he had a big patch of bald skin over his entire right hip. No fur there at all—just pink, creepy squirrel skin. It still gives me goosebumps to think about it. It's probably why he was hanging out at our bird feeder ... alone. Who'd invite an ugly thing like him to their nest for coffee?

He acted normal, though—or, at least, what I assumed was normal for a squirrel, eagerly scavenging the seeds that careless finches and sparrows had dumped onto the ground below. Clever dude, making those birds do all the work.

Soon, though, that wasn't good enough for him. Although the feeder was hanging from a large metal "S" hook dangling from a thin, half-dead twig that looks like it's still attached to the tree if you look at it just right, ol' Baldy decided he'd had enough waiting for leftovers to hit the ground and went right to the source of the food by climbing out on that branch and dropping head-first onto the top of the bird feeder.

He really should have consulted an engineer before these attempts, though (which were surprisingly numerous), because the weight of one large, overfed urban squirrel doesn't balance out well with a dead stick cracking off the end of another dead twig supposedly still part of an old tree. In a stiff breeze. He skittered up the stick, backing up all the way till he hit a branch big enough not to sway dangerously any time a chickadee breathed on it.

Within a few days of watching Baldy try to get at the way-too-expensive-for-big-squirrels bird seed, I decided to distract him and keep him on the ground by opening the back door and tossing out a few loose peanuts from a can of what Walmart calls "party peanuts." I wasn't sure whether the squirrel belonged to any sort of little squirrel fraternity or even *liked* to party, but if he did, I figured he'd be all set now, especially if I could find a way to toss him some tequila, a salt shaker, and a lime. And a few aspirin if he came back in the morning.

He sniffed the peanuts and passed them up for more of the seeds, but the birds loved them. I wasn't winning this battle with nature, but I wasn't easily deterred. If watching a fat, bald squirrel (I expected to see a comb-over on his little head and a little squirrel La-Z-Boy somewhere near the tree) had taught me anything, it was that there was never a reason to give up so soon. And at least I wasn't hanging out at the end of a dead twig.

I marched back into the house and raided the pantry for something he'd like. Anything to keep him away from the bird seed, which was about ten bucks for ten pounds and which was disappearing faster than a deadbeat dad on Father's Day. In a huff, I grabbed the bag of pecan halves I used for yummy pies I'm not allowed to eat myself. *I'll teach that little rodent,* I thought, as I broke a few of the halves in half (making them pecan quarters, if my math is correct) and tossed them out the back door and on the ground in the Foraging Frenzy area.

He grabbed the first pawful and ate it so fast I thought he was going to start choking. I wondered fleetingly if the Heimlich maneuver on a squirrel would mean using just my thumbs or if I'd accidentally brush up against that gross bald spot on his hip. The second pecan he carried off to the side of the house, where he buried it hastily in our long, still-unmown grass.

Meanwhile, I had gotten out my husband's engineering calculator and was rapidly finding that the squirrel was eating pecans that cost about $20 a pound. Yup, I sure fooled him. But at least he was ignoring the bird seed, which was about a dollar a pound.

Within days I'd created a monster. He was now prancing onto our back porch, sitting just a few feet outside the screen door, on his hind legs with his front paws clasped one over the other, like some pathetic orphan from *Oliver Twist*. I half expected him to start singing "Food, Glorious Food!" Shameful, really, for what was supposed to be a wild animal. Apparently, in the teeming metropolis of New Brighton, there isn't any such thing as a truly wild animal.

By now Baldy was responding to the sound of my voice. If he was in the Foraging Frenzy area while I was doing dishes, and I yelled to him out the back door, he'd end up on the porch waiting for his "hit" of gourmet pecan halves, which I fed to him one at a time to make them last a little longer. This critter was developing a mighty expensive habit, and I was his pusher. Except that pushers usually got paid, and I was getting squat. Literally I was getting squat, since he'd squat on the porch and eat those pecans inches from me and now didn't even bother to bury them. I think he gave up burying them when the other squirrel, the shrew, and the crazy hyperactive chipmunk saw where he was putting them. Really, he had to come up with better hiding places than six inches from the tree. I suspect this is one reason why squirrels will probably never rule the world. And by "probably," I mean "absolutely."

It took another month, but eventually Baldy began army-crawling up to me to take a pecan right from my hand. And, since his fur had grown back by then, I changed his name to Boldy.

As of this writing, he hasn't really noticed the name change. As long as the pecans keep coming, I bet he'd let me call him Nancy.

"You've Just Won ... A Brand New Car!"

By the time I was forty-nine years old, I had finally hit that stage of success in life where I was the envy of all of my friends. Well, perhaps not *all* of my friends. I mean, I have some friends who are on the *New York Times* bestseller list and some who are ten years older than I am and can wear Spanx in public without anyone laughing at them or throwing up. But, the envy of ... well, *some* of my friends. Okay, one, maybe, on a good day.

Why the envy? Because, yes, I finally owned a brand new car. It's mostly plastic inside (and outside, probably, though I admit I don't have much inclination to test that theory), and it's kinda small (or so says my 6′4″

husband whenever he has to sit in it), but everything in it was new when I first drove it home. Well, mostly new, since it mysteriously already had a "2" on the odometer, which I have never fully reconciled myself to over the three years I've had it. Who drove that thing for two miles in the month or two it had been sitting on the lot? Because even the test drive I took lasted at least five miles. Did one of the employees sneak into the place at night, grab a few sets of keys, and joyride around the parking lot for no apparent reason? The mind reels. Well, *my* mind reels. Then again, my mind reels a lot anyway—I don't need something as trite as who was driving my semi-new car to get my mind reeling.

So, to recap and get back on track: In June 2010, at age forty-nine, I was the proud owner of a Chevrolet Cobalt. Naturally, Chevrolet decided to stop making Cobalts that year and started making a better midsize car, the Cruze. And now I see Chevy Cruzes all over the road, mocking me for driving that ancient model Cobalt from 2010. And here I was, all excited to be driving a car with a remote starter that actually works. I can never catch a break.

One of the perks of buying a new car, instead of raiding the kids' piggy banks for coins to buy a used car with an 8-track player in the dashboard and bubble gum from the Carter Administration stuck to the passenger seat, is that it comes with a few free state inspections and oil changes. When the Cobalt was due for its first Pennsylvania inspection, I took it back to the dealership where we'd bought it.

For decades before this, I'd gotten used to taking dilapidated jalopies to the local greasy mechanic for inspections and sitting by the phone at home all day waiting for that ugly phone call where the mechanic breaks the news to me that he'll need to replace everything under the hood except the windshield washer reservoir—and even that looks a little iffy.

So, now, here I sit in the air-conditioned dealership waiting room, using their free WiFi and drinking their complimentary coffee (which isn't half bad), watching the big screen TV from a nicely padded seat around a little table I have all to myself. Even the fact that they can inspect the car fast enough for me to wait for it in their waiting room is new to me. I'd never waited for a car to be inspected because it just takes too long to catalog everything that's wrong with any car I've ever owned, and besides, the greasy mechanic doesn't even have a waiting room. He has two old kitchen dinette chairs, with most of the vinyl seat padding ripped off, sitting up against one wall in the small entryway where he has the cash register and a countertop, where once a year I write him the big checks and weep—a sort of yearly ritual between us.

Plus, the mechanic's floor is sticky and the window behind the two chairs is filthy, but at least the grime blocks out the sunlight in the summer. There's a penny candy machine (well, more accurately, a quarter candy machine) with candy I'm pretty sure they stopped making in the mid-'80s, and a sign on the wall behind the cash register that says, "Our service manager is

Helen Waite. So if you don't like our service, you can go to Helen Waite."

But the new Chevrolet dealership doesn't have a rude sign full of attitude or gumball machines full of bacteria. It has charming signs with good grammar, signs that thank me for my patience and understanding as they work feverishly on my car and ask me nicely not to smoke in the waiting room so we can all live happier, longer, and more productive lives. I feel as if I am in the waiting room for heaven and that St. Peter will show up with a long, flowing white robe and a clipboard, calling out my name and telling me that the Cobalt is allowed to come with me into Paradise. (Really, though, as much as I love the new Cobalt, if it's going to be paradise, it should be, like, a Mercedes, at least, right?)

And then, as if announcing I have just become a new father, a neat and tidy "mechanic" wearing a dark blue uniform with his name sewn over the breast pocket comes out to tell me the Cobalt is ready. I know he's not really one of the mechanics. He's a customer service rep. I can tell because his fingernails are cleaner and in nicer shape than mine (I must get the name of his salon before I leave), and he doesn't have grease stains anywhere. He's carrying a clipboard and very nearly breaks into song to tell me the Cobalt has passed inspection. I glance around furtively for Julie Andrews or Andrew Lloyd Webber.

I don't see either one of them in the waiting room, so I rise to get my keys from Anthony Newley The

Customer Service Rep. He hands them over cheerily, takes my paltry little check to cover the inspection, and I head for the door, where they have already brought my car around.

I get into the driver's seat of the newly vacuumed interior (which smells vaguely of fragrant peppermint, for some reason), and as I swing my left foot in, I glance at the ground.

Is that a yellow brick road?

Gee! P.S.

We've been married for nearly fourteen years, and I'm still not used to how my husband's brain works. Or sometimes, even THAT it works. Such is the healthy skepticism with which one enters a second marriage, I suppose. Or, any marriage with an engineer. (In reality, my secret wish is that his brain would take a few hours off. Just once.)

For my birthday a few years ago, Wayne inexplicably bought me a GPS. I say "inexplicably" because I hadn't previously expressed any interest in one, and he, on the other hand, had been drooling over them in the Best Buy for several years. Happy birthday, Wayne—I mean, *me*.

Although I initially scratched my head at this unusual gift, it soon became an indispensable part of my road trip paraphernalia, right up there with my suitcase, a Big Gulp of Diet Mountain Dew and an iPod with Talking Heads' "Road to Nowhere."

Having felt I had already let technology take a huge leap forward when I went from crayon-scribbled directions over the phone a week ahead of time to MapQuest, I found the leap from MapQuest to the GPS more than a little jarring. Instead of reaching for the MapQuest printout in 8-point Helvetica, with steps 3 through 6 inadvertently missing, a small device that looked like a big smartphone was talking at me from the dashboard. When you're used to taking long road trips alone, a sudden second voice in the car with you is enough to make you run your car off the road into a ditch. But at least you'll know exactly where the ditch is. If you've updated your GPS maps recently, that is. If not, you're on your own.

Once I got used to the contraption, I used it more often. But it's old enough that it didn't come standard with lifetime maps, as most do now. And I was enough of a skinflint to not shell out $70 the next year for new maps. After all, as my brother-in-law insisted, "Roads don't change, right?"

Well, apparently, even if the road itself stays in the same spot, it still finds a way to change. Sometimes, in western Pennsylvania, roads are renamed from US Route 60 South to Interstate 376 East. I can understand a road being upgraded from a US route to an interstate, but how did the road go from north-south to east-west? It's in exactly the same spot it was last year. The old, un-updated GPS insists to this day that the road is north-south, and I gotta side with the GPS on this one.

In related news, apparently the government sometimes builds completely new roads, to completely new places. New housing developments spring up, and they take the time and trouble to pave roads leading up to every house. And, they name those roads. Individually.

And if any of my friends ever move there, I'll never be able to find them because my GPS will lead me to a two-dimensional version of an open field nearby and then tell me to "when possible, make a legal U-turn."

Although I keep the GPS in my car's console, it's also good for hiking. I didn't know it had this feature, since I never walk anywhere on purpose unless I have to get something at the other end of my walk. Like, my shoes upstairs. Or the laundry in the basement.

I discovered this GPS feature by mistake when I turned it on and tapped a wee corner of the screen by accident. Seems I had, without knowing it, pushed the button that was going to tell me the walking distance to my next destination. So, when I tapped in the address of my sons' house forty miles away, the GPS announced my estimated time of arrival as 1,267 hours.

I panicked and thought they had been deported to Timbuktu.

Wayne began to ask me every day if I was using the

GPS. And I mean every day. Even when I was driving just to the grocery store a half-mile away. Or the post office, which is prit-near a mile from the house. I mean, I'm almost as big a gadget geek as he is, but there are limits to my geekiness. Then again, I did learn that the off-ramp of a nearby highway actually has a name like a regular road. Not that I remember now what it is. And not that I'll ever call it by name. I don't think the *Jeopardy* questions get that specific.

Still, I humored Wayne a little while longer before yanking the thing off the dashboard and putting it back in the console until the next road trip ... which, according to the GPS, will be about 336 hours from now.

Dear Mr. Chevrolet ...

MEMORANDUM

To: Mark Reuss, G.M. of General Motors, and Supreme Being in charge of Chevrolet products and vehicles:

On June 29, 2010, an event of epic proportions in the history of the human race occurred: I took ownership of my very first brand-new car. It was one of yours – a 2010 Chevrolet Cobalt – well, not one of yours personally, of course. That would be grand theft auto, and I certainly wouldn't be writing to you about it so openly if that were the case. We signed the papers and took it home honestly. Honest.

Anyway, back to my original reason for writing to you. I want to thank you for making such a fine automobile. I realize I may not be the best judge of new automobiles, having never owned one until last June at age forty-nine and having gotten a mild case of hives in the dealership while signing that big check and the financing papers. But, it's a compliment all the same.

I'll never forget the moment I got into the Cobalt for the first time, to take it for a test drive. The car started flawlessly and purred like a happy kitten. I noticed that the odometer read "2." Two? Seriously? This is the first time I've owned a car that registered its mileage in anything lower than five digits (six, with the decimal).

Later, after the Cobalt was officially ours and I was driving it home, I began to wonder about that "2." My first thought was, "HEY! Who's been driving MY CAR without my permission?" My second thought was, "I'm already driving a used car." I tried not to let that get me down.

But again, back to my main reason for this letter: I am in love with my new/now-used Cobalt. Granted, someone could have bought me a roller skate with a four-cylinder engine and an odometer at "0" and I would have been almost as thrilled, but let's not get caught up in semantics.

The only "down" side to having bought a Cobalt from your fine company is that, about a week later, my husband asked to borrow it. You must understand that my husband is 6′4″ and built like a linebacker, and your Cobalt—well, frankly, is not. But, his gargantuan

Sierra pickup truck had to go into the shop for inspection, and it was either lend him the Cobalt or get up at 4:30 in the morning to take him to work myself and then go back eight hours later to pick him up. Letting him borrow it seemed a small sacrifice to make at the time...

...Until that morning, when he asked me for the keys to the Cobalt and walked out into the early morning darkness. I stood on the front porch in my bathrobe and slippers, sniffling, holding back the tears and waving good-bye as if I were sending a child off for the first day of kindergarten. My husband saw me weeping and waving and waved back. Poor fool thought I was missing him already.

I don't mean to underestimate my adoration and love for him, but never, *ever* underestimate a middle-aged woman in sudden possession of a car with four matching wheel covers, four cup holders, two electrical ports, and six months of free satellite radio. And yes, when my husband got home that evening, I sneaked out into the driveway to make sure he hadn't dented anything. A girl can never be too careful.

And, yes, I also checked the odometer. It was already in triple digits. Perhaps it's time to trade it in. What have you got in a shiny, new roller skate?

Random Thoughts

Sometimes when I'm taking notes for future essays, I end up with a bunch of dregs that just don't warrant an entire essay (and I realize that could be said of most of the full essays in this book, but let's not belabor the point). That's when I give up and just glop them all together into one piece of random thoughts, each bit its own nugget of wisdom. Get in, get out, nobody gets hurt. Usually.

* **If you use** one of the larger kitchen trash cans, never dump cooked broccoli into the bottom of a new kitchen trash bag in the summer if you don't have air conditioning. Just a warning. Trust me.

* **During the first season** of the HBO series *The Sopranos,* Tony and Carmella Soprano had about twenty-seven different bathrobes. Is that a fact-check error on the part of the show, or were we supposed to notice this and think how outrageously wealthy they were?

* **There is a product** called Mister Steamy. It's a little plastic ball in which you put water and then add it to your dryer load, supposedly to add steam and get out wrinkles. But I keep thinking: Don't you put the wet clothes into the dryer to get the extra water OUT? Isn't there already too much steam being generated by the clothes you're drying? What am I missing here?

* **Did you ever forget** you put on a T-shirt with a funny saying on it and then spend the rest of the day wondering why everyone is pointing at you and laughing? Or worse, did you then assume it was because of the funny T-shirt, only to discover you wore a simple polo shirt today?

* **I'm starting to realize** just how good household pets have it. When your dog or cat walks by, you instinctively reach over or down and pet them, rub their chins, scratch their backs ... and generally make them happy. Imagine how great it would be if we could walk by people we love and they'd reach out and give us back rubs and neck rubs every time! Some people pay $175 an hour for a massage, but your dog or cat gets 'em for free twenty times a day.

* **Did you ever take two slices of bread** out of the bag to make a sandwich, eat the whole sandwich, and then discover that the next three slices in the bag are moldy? Do you try really hard not to think about it too much?

* **I finally bought** my first pair of "cheater" glasses at Walmart. They're really just little magnifying glasses you can wear on your face. But years ago, when Wayne first noticed he had to find the "sweet spot" on a pill bottle or a newspaper ad in order to read it clearly, he bought an actual magnifying glass and keeps it on the end table next to the La-Z-Boy. At first it seemed like overkill, but I admit I'd started using it myself before buying the cheaters.

And when Wayne's brother Ed was trying to read some fine print one day, I offered him my cheaters, which were within reach next to my arm chair. He politely said no, so I offered him the magnifying glass instead. He lit up like a Christmas tree and grabbed it eagerly. Does it look like a power tool or something? It must be a guy thing. All I know is, I wanted to put one of those Sherlock Holmes houndstooth hats on him.

* **I assume a church** is about as nondenominational as you can get when I'm driving down the highway and see a sign for the "Exit 59 Church."

* **I've read somewhere** that you should use rice to dry out electronics (such as cell phones) that get wet. The tip is to put the phone into a zip-lock bag along with the dry, uncooked rice, and the rice will magically soak up the moisture and the phone will dry out. No clue if brown rice works better than white rice. So, I'm left to wonder: If you're in a hurry, is it faster to use minute rice?

I've Got the Blues

Going to an outdoor blues festival in Johnstown, Pa., with two other fifty-year-olds could have been depressing, even if we do like each other. For one thing, the place is nicknamed "Flood City." Who does that? Who nicknames their town after the worst disaster in its history? And yes, I know, it's a *blues* festival—by definition you're not supposed to be happy when you're singing the blues. Plus, we assumed we'd be the old fogeys of the crowd, and that alone would have given us the blues.

Turns out we were right around the middle of the age spectrum. The place was oozing with aging gray, ponytailed or bald accountants and hippies with long, scary, ZZ-Top beards, drinking hard lemonade and wearing beat-up leather baseball caps—turned backwards, of course. Everyone was wearing concert T-shirts from the '70s, and I felt out of place wearing a blouse and capris. At least I had the decency to wear an old pair of Birkenstocks.

The other end of the spectrum (though a far smaller number) contained twenty-somethings who were probably all conceived at similar blues festivals in the late '80s. I wasn't sure if they were there because singing the blues is still cool and hip or because there's really nothing else to do in Johnstown but visit the Flood Museum ... and the beer was cheap and plentiful.

Let's face it, though: Nobody likes to spend the day using Port-a-Potties after drinking warm, cheap beer all day. Except for my husband, Wayne, who apparently took it up as a hobby, judging from how many times he had to visit them. Good thing they had a few "Big and Tall" ones there for him.

Speaking of Port-a-Potties (and who doesn't love that?), the only time I allowed myself to use one that day, I was in line behind a very old lady (she probably got her first birthday cards on parchment scrolls). She was wearing a matching green pastel polyester pantsuit, low-slung strappy sandals, and a metric ton of costume jewelry, hair coiffed into place with half a can of hairspray. When it was her turn, she daintily stepped up to the nearest Port-a-Potty and tried to open the door, only to find it wouldn't budge. After a few hearty tugs with her tiny, wrinkled hands, she turned to me and sheepishly asked, "Is this stuck? Can you help me?"

I smiled and said gently, "You see that big red square next to the door handle? That means it's occupied and someone has locked the door from the inside. Look for one with a green square."

She was obviously a Port-a-Potty virgin (the wafting scent of stale perfume and the jangling of the beaded bracelets were dead giveaways), and she hadn't noticed the colored squares near the door handles. She thanked me and searched for a green-squared stall, tiptoeing over the puddles of mud from the afternoon's earlier rain. I was busy wondering how the person felt inside the stall she had been tugging on, worrying that the plastic mechanism wouldn't hold and that the door would swing open at any moment. If the woman had been at all robust, the results could have been far funnier—at least to me.

As it was, I quickly forgot about the old woman as I climbed inside a stall of my own and made sure the door handle was securely in the locked position before hovering myself over the horrifying open pit inside. We all know there are unimaginable monsters lurking inside that Port-a-Potty. Well, not *completely* unimaginable. When you're the one inside, trying not to notice the strange plastic echo any time you move or cough or let any sort of substance leave your body, you can most definitely imagine the monsters in the Port-a-Potty. Very, very clearly. Why, you can almost *hear* them, can't you? Slushing around down there, waiting till the count of four or maybe five before reaching up and yanking on anything blocking the little bit of light they get from the oval-shaped hole above their heads. One ... *(must get finished before the count of four)* ... two ... *(I had to pee like a race horse when I was standing in line outside, and now I can't seem to go at all!)* ... threeeeeee ... *(oh, good grief, I'm going to die in here, and I'll be on the six o'clock news when they send one of those news vans with the big satellite antenna on top)* ... fourrrrrr ... *(paper, paper, where's toilet paper? how fast can I wrap some around my hand and get out of here?)*

I just broke out into a cold sweat typing that last paragraph. Obviously I'm not quite over the whole harrowing Port-a-Potty experience. I suspect I'm suffering from PTSD (post-tinkle stress disorder).

Whatever this feeling is, it'll be a long time before I attend another blues festival. Unless I buy myself a box of Depends first. And, judging from the age of half the crowd there last time, I probably won't be the only one wearing them.

Mutual of Pennsylvania's Wild Kingdom

I fear I have inadvertently started a wildlife sanctuary in my back yard at the new house. The likelihood of this happening was close to nil when spring hit, because we now live in an old Victorian house right on the main street of town. Traffic zooms by the front of the house at all hours—Medic Rescue ambulances, police cars, pickup trucks—and there's a railway line about a block farther away, parallel to that main drag. Nothing says rural solitude like a freight train rattling the 130-year-old windows at two in the morning.

A few things have given the wildlife a false sense of security in my main-street neighborhood:

• **We all have our yards completely enclosed** in high wooden privacy fences, and all that's missing to make this place a zoo is a ticket booth out front by the gate and some polar bears. (I'll wait for winter here, and then double-check for the polar bears.)

• **We are virtually petless,** and the neighbors on both sides of us have boisterous, opinionated dogs—scary, vile, nasty monsters who would rip the front legs off a squirrel in two seconds flat. Well, perhaps I exaggerate and have just voiced the squirrels' opinion instead of my own. I like dogs. I just don't want to see them gnawing on squirrel-leg in my back yard.

• **Our lawn mower has decided** to opt for early retirement, without taking a little time to let us train his replacement. We've threatened to withhold his pension and medical benefits, but that hasn't deterred him. So, our entire half-acre of grass is teeming with snakes and creepy-crawlies I'd rather not see before they bite me with their foul venom.

Whatever their reasons, all the critters are here. It started with the birds, who were completely welcome when the snow melted and the flowers began to bloom. A pair of cardinals, some chickadees, two separate pairs of mourning doves that nested in our bedroom window sill, several blue jays, a host of robins, some finches, and sparrows as far as the eye could see. (In my case, the eye can't see all that far anymore, but I meant someone else's eye.)

The robin took all spring and summer to figure out how to build a nest in our back porch rafters without the whole thing collapsing like the poorly built balcony of a seedy third-world night club. Her eggs have just hatched, and I swear I don't see how these chicks are going to survive getting out of that nest. They're wedged up in those rafters so tightly there's no way they'll be able to fly out of that nest. I don't want to be around when they splat on my porch in a few weeks. Maybe I'll throw a patio chair cushion under the nest. Wayne, ever the animal lover, wants to knock it down with a broom. But, that robin's worked so hard to get that nest up there that I'm willing to live and let splat.

A few months ago I began to get paranoid, sitting at my little desk in the piano room, hearing a strange sort of tapping at the windows. It was persistent, but when I jumped up to catch whatever neighbor had a sick sense of humor to tap on our windows, I'd find no one. As soon as I'd sit back down to pay more bills, the tapping would start again.

Since I'm fairly sure male cardinals aren't usually rabid, the one whose nest is somewhere near my windows must just be insane. The tapping went on constantly for days before I caught the cardinal in the act. He was flying from the dogwood tree outside the windows and landing on the outside sill, tapping on the glass with his beak and batting on the glass with his wings. Over and over again. One evening this happened every five minutes for nearly four hours straight. Sometimes I wish I had that kind of focus and persistence, minus the insanity. Writing often feels that way—as if I am banging my head against a window for hours on end for no reason and with no discernible result, except the pounding headache and upset stomach.

A little Facebook questioning and internet searching revealed that cardinals can be quite territorial and never quite learn that the reflection of a cardinal they're seeing in a window is simply a reflection and not another cardinal trying to raid their territory. As beautiful as these birds are, their egos far outweigh their brains, and some will not stop this self-destructive behavior for their entire lives once begun. The worst part in this cardinal's case is that we have fifteen windows on the first floor alone. And just when he might have taken a breather, attacking his reflection in only *some* of our first-floor windows, we started remodeling the bathroom and took out a six-foot wall mirror, placing it (you guessed it) on the back porch across from one of the dining room windows.

So, Mr. Cardinal would now fly to that window sill, beat up his evil twin, then turn to fly away ... only to see what he perceived as an even more stunning cardinal than the ones he was *almost* seeing in the window. He'd fly to the mirror propped up against the porch railing, stand on the porch in front of it, and beat the living daylights out of that two-dimensional usurper for hours at a time. I'd have felt sorry for him if he wasn't obviously such an arrogant idiot about it.

We'd also put some metal shelving out on the back

porch while we were in the process of moving and unpacking, and his wife would sit on the shelving, in between the dining room window and the propped-up mirror, watching her husband flit back and forth from sill to mirror and back, beating up first one rude interloper and then another.

And yet, the two intruders persisted every bit as long as he did. Meanwhile, his wife sat on the shelving, her head on a swivel, watching him bob and weave for as long as she could stand to watch his stupidity. Once in a while she'd chirp or make some noise, and I can only assume she was saying, "Carl! He's still there! Get him, Carl! What kind of slacker are you? Mother was right about you. You'll never amount to anything if you can't stand up to a pair of scrawny guys like these two! Carl!"

Nag nag nag ...

I was about to chastise Wayne for leaving that five-foot mirror on the back porch for so long, but I caught myself before I started to nag. Seems we're not so different from the animals after all.

Attack of the 50-Square-Foot Bathroom (Day 47)

It's starting to wear thin. To be honest, it started to wear thin around Day 3, but nobody noticed but me because Wayne hid all the calendars for some strange reason. Well, the reason was strange on Day 3, but now that it's Day 47, with no end in sight, I understand why he hid the calendars. Once he starts consulting the Mayans, I'll know we're in big trouble. Oh, who am I kidding? We've been in big trouble since Day 1.

The bathroom demolition has ended, along with no small piece of my sanity. Most of the bits and pieces of debris made it out of the house all right and now sit harmlessly in the driveway. Whenever I come home from an errand, I have to be careful not to pull too far into the driveway so I don't hit a stray nail or bolt or toilet lying there. The toilet's been the easiest to avoid so far.

Despite the fact that this project has no end date and I'm learning a little bit more about the theological concept of eternity with each passing week, Wayne has optimistically bought most of the fixtures we'll eventually be using in the remodeled bathroom. We recently made an exciting trip to Home Depot to pick out a vanity, a medicine cabinet, a toilet, and even the shower stall, and all the excitement of finishing such an awesome project seemed real for about ten or twelve seconds before reality hit me: We don't have a garage or tool shed, so all these fixtures are going to have to find a temporary home somewhere else. The bathroom is nowhere near ready to put them in—we've discovered issue after issue with the flooring, the subflooring, the previous walls, the previous insulation … and now the room is stripped back to the bare studs. (And please, no jokes about "stripping" and "bare studs," okay? This is a family-friendly book.)

I swear I can see the siding through one gap between the studs, and is that daylight coming through that gaping hole? I no longer want to hear project updates at dinner because I fear they'll include which forest creatures have found their way in through the wide-open heating vent that seems to lead to the back yard instead of the basement. I know I am hearing crickets echoing through that vent once it gets dark. Wayne brushes my fears aside as silly, but I start wishing the room still had a door on it to close at night while we're sleeping. I wonder just how big a raccoon has to get before it won't fit through the vent opening. I'm sleeping with one eye open from now on, just in case. And maybe I'm sleeping with one eye open *in the car*.

After a few days, I find I don't really mind the four-foot shower stall sitting in the driveway, except that it'll be autumn soon and the leaves from the tree right above it will start collecting in the shower pan. I'm pretty sure raking a shower stall just isn't what the manufacturer had in mind and we will void the warranty the first time we try it. What I do mind, though, are the toilet and sink sitting in my living room. Some of this is a matter of perspective, I realize, since both items are still in their original boxes and are, conveniently, the height of a typical end table. I throw a table cloth over them and make do, for now. After all, we don't entertain that often, although now I'm starting to understand why. And not having a functional bathroom is only part of the problem.

There are rumors that the room will have a subfloor again today, but I brush these rumors aside as silly. I've heard these rumors before, on Day 27 and then again on Day 35. Besides, I'm kind of getting used to the earthy aroma of the dirt that sits below the joists and the subflooring. When it rains, the smell of mud caresses my senses while I'm trying to make dinner two rooms away. It figures we're remodeling one of only two rooms that don't sit over the basement, rooms that were added separately in the 1950s. The terms "flush" and "level" and "plumb" and "straight" are jokes to us now. (Let's face it: "Flush" is funny for a bunch of reasons when you're remodeling a bathroom.) This room looks like it was engineered by Willy Wonka on a bad sugar buzz.

I hear some random cursing wafting from the bathroom as the men work. No subflooring today. There is no joy in Mudville.

Weed-Whacking as a Cardio Workout

If you want a good workout and plenty of exercise, you could join a public gym or exercise club for thirty bucks a month or more. If you're an old, flabby woman like I am and are intimidated by other people in a public gym or exercise club, you could join Curves instead, which is really just a place for old, flabby women to hang out together for half an hour, telling jokes about their husbands while gasping for breath on non-threatening exercise machines. (Don't ask what the "Curves" refers to. Let's just say it's not what most men hope it is.)

And, if spending your hard-earned money on a gym membership just doesn't seem worth it in the long run, but you still want the benefit of that kind of exercise, I highly recommend what works for me: namely, waiting until it's nearly summer to bother cutting the grass on your half-acre yard, so that it's waist high and you need to use a weed-whacker because you'd ruin any lawn mower you tried to use on it—either that, or you'd just lose the lawn mower in the overgrowth and not find it until someone trips over it or until global warming melts the polar ice caps so your yard is underwater and a reef starts to grow on it.

I inadvertently came across this little known cardio/aerobic exercise secret this year when we moved into our new house, which boasts about five times the yard space as our previous house. Well, perhaps "boasts" is a bit ambitious since neither Wayne nor I want to admit it's our yard yet, let alone boast about it. Our lawn mower curled up and died as soon as the weather got warm, as if to tell us, "Oh, no you don't! I didn't mind the tenth of an acre I had to tackle every other week because your yard was so bad the grass refused to grow. But this half-acre monstrosity where you live now is just *not* in my contract. Talk to my agent. I'll be in my dressing room."

Freakin' prima donna. That's what we get for buying it on sale with a coupon and a few leftover gift cards. Even threatening to dump it off at the Goodwill and replace it with a proper John Deere tractor couldn't get it to work right. We're having Wayne's mechanically gifted brother Brian look at it for us, and I won't be surprised if he comes back with a diagnosis of clinical depression—for the mower, of course, not for him.

In the meantime, though, the grass has not stopped growing. Funny how that happens: Rain falls (in Pittsburgh, in the spring—this is not news); grass grows; more rain falls; more grass grows, even as neighbors on all sides of us get out lawn mowers and keep their grass at a respectable ankle height. At first, I wondered if there was some sort of western Pennsylvania native dance for stopping the rain, but even if there was, I was never going to pull it off, standing in the middle of my yard with some ridiculous outfit on, bellowing incantations with inappropriate inflections and dancing with my two left feet, probably twisting an ankle in my higher-than-ankle-height grass in the process. It's a shame, really, because that would have been good exercise too, and a mighty funny comedy routine for the neighbors.

So, a full two months after everyone else in town had started manicuring their lawns, I had a decision to make. With our mower in a virtual coma (and us ready to pull the literal plug on the thing), but with no inclination to buy a new mower just yet (hope springs eternal—and the credit card balance does not), I was left with only one choice: I was going to have to weedwhack the entire yard. And, like just about every other story in this book, it seemed like a good idea at the time.

Then I started thinking about it a little too much. It started with an innocent comment from my parents about wearing protective gear: long pants, closed-toe shoes, safety goggles, perhaps a HAZMAT suit if

I could find one at the thrift store in my size.... And now that the conversation had gone there, I couldn't keep my mind off all the things that could go wrong in a project this size. Wait, no, things that would *most definitely* go wrong. I'd lived long enough on this earth and done enough foolhardy projects in my lifetime to know that my husband's optimistic personal motto of "What could possibly go wrong?" is always rhetorical, naïve, and downright stupid, especially when ***I*** ask it. At that point I'm just asking for trouble.

Although I might have predicted the trouble would start with the weed-whacker itself*, the thing worked like a charm. Well, not exactly a charm. If it had worked like a charm, I could have just waved a magic wand and wished the grass away, and of course, that's just silly. (But don't think I didn't try it, just to be sure. And getting the wand away from that Potter kid was tricky, let me tell you.)

But, at least these little contraptions have vastly improved since their early days in the 1970s when I had to use the newfangled version to trim around all the fences and brick patios and railroad ties and dog pens and garages and sidewalks in the yard where I grew up. You know, back when you had to bump them on the ground every few seconds to get more string, which always felt like you were slapping someone upside the head to bully him on the playground at recess:

---

*I suppose the more correct generic term for this lawn equipment is "line trimmer," but "weed-whacker" sounds so much funnier.

"Give me more string or I'll take your lunch money and bonk you on the head!"

"Wait… what?" ... *bonk* ... "Hey! Ouch!"

"I said, more string, or I swear I'll do it again. And this time I'll give you a wedgie too. Don't make me have to throttle your brain around."

"I'm feeding you string as fast as I—" ... *bonk* ... "Ow! Quit it!"

"Listen, you idiot. If I don't get more string in five seconds, I'm going to bump you into next week."

"All right, all right! Oh crap, I think I'm out of str—"

... *bonk bonk* ...

Silence.

"Dad! the weed-whacker's busted again!"

Meanwhile, thirty-five years later, we now have access to wonderful weed-whackers that do all manner of once-impossible tasks. Oh sure, I'll be far more impressed when it can brew a decent pot of coffee while I'm doing the yard work, or better still, when ***I*** can brew a decent pot of coffee while ***it's*** doing the yard work. But for now, I'm grateful that I don't have to abuse the poor thing by smacking it against the ground every five seconds. "Auto-feed" is my new favorite word.

Once I donned the makeshift hermetically sealed spacesuit made from duct tape and spare bike parts (my personal homage to the guys on Apollo 13), made out a living will, and asked for prayer on our church's prayer chain, I was ready to begin the weed-whack proper. I took the GPS from the car and stuffed it into my back pocket just in case and ventured out into the back yard.

The duct tape around my armpits chafed a little bit, and the GPS kept trying to recalculate and send me into the neighbor's yard (I suspect it just wanted to get away from me as fast as possible), but the HAZMAT suit was a perfect fit. I'd spray-painted the generic Ugg boots with WD-40 to keep the gigantic poisonous snakes from climbing up my legs. It wasn't until hours later that I remembered that WD-40 is probably flammable and I shouldn't have been using gas-powered equipment around it. I avoided lighting any matches, tried not to look too closely at the grass near my legs, and hacked down half the yard before collapsing into a sweaty puddled heap in the middle of the yard.

My husband found me lying there the following Tuesday, but I think that might have been because I'd missed my weekly grocery trip and we'd run out of Dorito's.

I bought myself a Curves membership the very next day and never looked back.

Head-Wound-of-the-Month Club

If you used my childhood medical history as a guide, you'd have reported my parents to Child Protective Services, if they even had such a thing back when I was a kid. I had this uncanny ability to force my parents to take me on a yearly pilgrimage to the emergency room. It wasn't out of a sense of curiosity, or even because I someday hoped to intern there as a medical student. And I wasn't donating blood, unless you call the A-positive flowing freely from one of my appendages (usually my head) and onto an old washcloth a donation. Which I didn't. Nobody was saving this stuff. My mom was usually rinsing it out of the washcloth and down the kitchen sink as if she were an army medic on the front lines.

You see, I'm a natural-born klutz. Nobody else in my

family seems to be as clumsy as I am, so it must be some sort of ultra-recessive gene that only I got. Sometimes I wonder if joining Ancestry.com will turn up some faded scanned document listing past relatives who were as clumsy as I am. Perhaps a great-great uncle died when he stepped on a banana peel or caught his left shoelace under his right shoe while he was casually walking down the street one day, minding his own business. You'd think an action like minding your own business would be fairly safe and worry-free, but not for a klutz. For a natural-born klutz, even getting up out of a chair can be hazardous to one's health. It's why I eye all seating options suspiciously to this very day.

As a child and young teen, I began to suspect I was different from the other children because I was the only one with a special washcloth that my mom used to stanch the ungodly flow of blood from my chin or knee or forehead or chin or elbow or wrist or chin (I had to count my chin at least three times because that's how many times I gashed it open over the years). I can still picture that washcloth—a pale, pastel green, thinning and threadbare but perfect for wrapping around a plastic sandwich bag filled with ice cubes and then holding against whatever the wound-of-the-month was.

Nearly all of my E.R.-worthy wounds were on my head ... and if you've ever met me, you'll know that explains a lot. I developed a sort of pattern: About every other year the head wound would occur on my chin. Once I fell off my brand-new bike ("brand-new" meaning my parents had just bought it that very day) and my chin hit the street before the rest of me. Once I fell in my uncle's finished basement and my chin made contact with a pipe along the floor. Once I ... well, I can't even remember how I got the third chin wound. I chalk that up to memory loss from the first two times I gashed my chin open. Besides, by this point the emergency room doctors were ready to forgo stitches for a zipper so they could just zip it back up the next time I opened my chin on concrete. Peter Boyle had nuthin' on me.

Twice I gashed my forehead. Well, that's not exactly true. Only one of those times was my fault. Once I landed forehead-first on the corner of a concrete step at a car dealership while my parents were wheeling and dealing. Definitely my fault, although I think they got a great deal on that Mustang after that. The pity factor was worth a few hundred bucks.

But the other time my brother hit me with a hammer. To this day my parents both swear it was mostly accidental ... but I keep keying in on that word "mostly." And people wonder why I dislike home improvement projects. I still keep a close eye on my brother when we're together. I just never know when he might want to exact a little more childhood revenge, even if it is forty-five years later. Some wounds run deeper than any washcloth can cover. He's probably still bitter that I got to be the goody-two-shoes of the family, and he was stuck being the hip, cool sibling.

I was getting all these assorted head wounds during an era when nobody really cared if you ended up with scars on your otherwise stunning face (or *my* face, whichever the case may be). When a kid's wailing on the table in the E.R., her face covered with this strange sheet with a hole cut in it that would have creeped out even the Elephant Man, well, you don't pay nearly as much attention to the finer points of facial stitches. Just use the black, thick catgut, and get it done before the Novocaine wears off.

And so, the scar above my right eyebrow (from the concrete step at the car dealership) resembles this strange, freakish shelf when I raise my eyebrows or otherwise look surprised. It didn't help that they used those old, thick, black Frankenstein stitches. Did they also have to experiment with creating steppes and plains on my face? Was the doctor drunk or just mad at my parents for some reason? Or both? Maybe he'd just put in a lower offer on that Mustang.

That scar is one of the main reasons I prefer to wear my hair with bangs. But, at least I managed to land on that concrete corner at just the right spot to miss poking my eye out entirely. And yes, I know I probably just creeped you out. That was kinda my goal. Some people prefer to flaunt their achievements and accomplishments. Since I'm still working on those, I instead prefer to show off my stupidity and clumsiness, with a dash of my many brushes with death thrown in—like almost drowning in the shower in my forties, tripping and falling UP the steps in my thirties, totaling my mom's Ford Pinto at fifteen miles per hour in my teens ... you know, all the things that attest to my adventurous, bold lifestyle.

Because, you know, you only live once. But, you can trip and fall down many, many, *many* times.

Bats in My Belfry ... and My House

Bad things happen to good people. I've come to terms with this principle since I believe in original sin and the fall of mankind. There's nothing particularly funny about that doctrine, I admit, but since I wake up every morning painfully aware that any combination of weird stuff could happen to me, I'm not really surprised when it actually does. Oh sure, I'm upset, and I'm bummed, but I'm not surprised.

And so, when I got home from a week-long conference in Indiana—having received a short email the day before from my husband stating simply, "I trapped a bat on the third floor ... I think it was the only one, but there may be others"—I assumed he'd dealt with it while I was away and that the ugly situation was over … and it was now the stuff of stories he would tell me now that I was home.

We'd moved into our home about six weeks earlier, even though we hadn't finished remodeling the only full bathroom in the place. (And let's not bring up that painful subject again, okay?) We had a half-bath on the first floor that worked, but everyone knows "half-bath" really means "zero-shower/zero-bathtub." So, every morning or every evening, we'd each have to drive back to the old house a mile away to take a shower, toting clean clothing and toiletries. It felt like camping in a state park, where everyone uses communal gender-specific bath houses. But we didn't sink six figures into this new house so we could go camping. Heck, if I wanted to go camping, I'd sit out in the back yard with the snakes and the birds and the stink bugs. No, wait, the stink bugs are in the house. Pardon me.

The shower-jaunts wore thin a lot faster than I would have thought (being the eternal optimist that I am, of course), and that evening in late July when I got back from my week-long conference and Wayne headed out to take his nightly shower was the last straw. I curled up on the sofa with my laptop and figured I'd check out Facebook while waiting for him to come back.

I glanced up just in time to see a winged creature the size of a pterodactyl heading straight for my face at breakneck speed. Well, perhaps I exaggerate. Perhaps it was a small bat that weighed an ounce or two, and perhaps it was really just circling the room up near the twelve-foot ceilings before heading to another room. Perhaps.

In any case, I—being bat-phobic to the point of abject hysteria—became abjectly hysterical. I shrieked at the now-panic-stricken bat, "Go away! Leave me ALONE!" and I did the only logical thing a person could do: I hoisted the laptop up over my head like it was a little roof. My bumpy head was hitting keys on the keyboard as I tried to pull the laptop down farther so it would completely cover my semi-round head. (Note: This will not keep bats from attacking you if they really have their hearts set on it, but the shrieking can be very effective at the right sustained pitch and length.) The bat never got near me.

I mustered as much bravery as I could and poked one small hand outside the safety of the laptop-tent to reach for the cordless phone on the end table next to me. That eight inches felt like a mile as I plucked the handset off the cradle and pulled it up under the laptop-tent. My hands shook as I dialed Wayne's cell phone number and waited as it rang and rang and rang and ...

"Hello?"

"AAAEEIIIIIIRRAAAIAIIIIIIGGHHHHHH!"

"Linda?"

I ever so briefly took offense at the fact that he knew it was me because I was shrieking.

"The bat! It's still here! Come back! Come back!"

"But I haven't showered yet."

"I don't care if you're stinky and dirty, come back!"

To his credit, he came right home to deal with the bat. He opened every window, every door, turned off most of the lights, and ran around the house shooing it with a broom, only to lose it somewhere on the second floor.

An hour later he announced, "It's probably gone," and went back to the old house to shower. I sat cowering on the sofa while he was away, pulling the pocket doors closed and vowing never to leave the living room again until I knew the bat was gone. Right about then I realized I had to use the bathroom ... which was about three rooms away. I found an old baseball hat, grabbed an afghan and threw it over myself like a cape, and army-crawled all the way to the bathroom, weeping. I am not kidding. I am really not kidding.

Then I realized: Wouldn't leaving windows and doors open just mean more bats could fly in? For an engineer, the man can be so irrational sometimes.

It took three days and three nights to get that bat to leave the house, the little freeloader. Turns out we had done everything wrong. We should have closed all the windows and opened only a single door, keeping lights on. A sort of airplane runway with landing lights for wayward bats. By this point I was ready to try anything. I'd barely slept. I'd hardly eaten. My nerves were shot. It felt like I was in college during finals week again.

As soon as we did the bat-runway things on that third night, the little guy whooshed down the main staircase, banked right and flew straight out the front door. Didn't even have the decency to say goodbye.

Internal Organs Have Feelings Too

I've become convinced that my internal organs all have a life of their own, and that they have clandestine weekly meetings in which they cast secret ballots (and ask for photo I.D.) and vote me off my own island. I'm also convinced, though, that my pancreas is voting more than once, and that my stomach has been disenfranchised and his vote conveniently gets lost due to some sort of organic hanging chad that is really just my appendix.

In any case, I know nearly all my organs hate me—except my stomach, with whom I am on intimate terms too many times a day, which isn't much of a secret to anyone who's seen me lately. As soon as I get out of bed—a circus feat of derring-do when it's 5′2″ me hoisting my petard out of a sloshy, low waterbed—I'm assaulted anew with the evidence: My body is revolting. And yes, I get the play on words there. And yes, I meant it both ways.

But let's stick with the meaning I started this thought with: The various parts of my body are all in league with the devil to conspire against me, to keep me from my appointed tasks for the day. Evil minions of Satan they are, from my brain right down to the heels of my too-small feet. Each one spends the hours in which I'm sleeping writing their dissertations on "Why Linda Needs to Suffer Tomorrow." The organ that wins that morning gets to torture me until lunchtime, when the runner-up takes over until dinner. After dinner, it's a virtual free-for-all of aches, pains, and strange, high-pitched gastric sounds that make small children whimper and find my husband covering his ears and asking, "Is there a whale loose in the house or something?" *Besides you, I mean, honey*…. I know he's thinking it. Might as well type it here.

Some people have irritable bowels. Others have spastic bladders. Me? I have an annoyed pancreas, a delirious stomach, an angry spleen, a miffed lower intestine, and a uterus that hasn't spoken to me in years except to remind me every month just how peeved it still is that I didn't have any babies smaller than nine pounds. Dear uterus: Get over it already. That was twenty years ago. Can't you just retire gracefully and leave me alone?

Some people have one organ failure at a time. I wouldn't wish a catastrophic single-organ collapse on myself, but at least I wouldn't have to multitask when trying to juggle the various parts of me that are all vying for my attention these days. No, I didn't step on something in the back yard; that's plantar fasciitis. No, I'm not blushing at an off-color joke; that's rosacea. And no, the congenital dislocated hip is not coming back to haunt me; that's me sitting at a desk all day with joints that are a half-century old and haven't been in for a tune-up in, well, okay, never.

I picture my organs like runners in an Olympic race: a relay team where one runs for a bit then tags a teammate to take over, who then later tags a third teammate just as he is losing energy. I haven't figured out if they take turns alphabetically, or if there is a sort of daily lottery like a Shirley Jackson story gone bad, but as soon as I fix one daily ailment or ache, a new one shows up. And apparently this relay team is going for the gold.

Oh sure, it makes life interesting to wonder what parts of me are going to hurt today—and maybe I should start taking bets like some sort of anatomical bookie. I can see family and friends lining up now to hand over their hard-earned cash:

"I'll put twenty bucks on your liver to start pumping out glucose by ten A.M."

"Fifteen dollars on the knees to give out the second time you climb the stairs today."

"Gimme twenty-five that your butt falls asleep in

the chair and you can't get up without wetting yourself."

Really, guys, the votes of confidence are a tad underwhelming. I may have to stop stuffing my face and start stuffing that ballot box instead.

Super Powers I Don't Want

Unlike every other normal human being, I'm not all that interested in having super powers. I don't aspire to ninjahood or superherohood. Motherhood has been enough of an adventure for me.

So, when I hear people answer that theoretical question, "What super powers would you want if you could have them?" I find myself flummoxed that they have enough presence of mind to answer it. They've been thinking about it. They've mulled over the various types of powers available (is there a list somewhere that I missed?), and they've come up with a Top Three (or Four or Five) and can immediately answer the question with intelligence and wit.

Meanwhile, there sits Linda, mouth hanging open slackjawed, unable to form a decent sentence fragment on the subject, let alone a philosophical discourse like everyone else in the room.

I finally decided it was time to get with the program and figure out which super powers I'd want if I had the choice (which apparently I don't, since every superhero I know just gets zapped with some power or other without filling out a form or completing a survey, making the exercise even more pointless than I had originally thought). Since I couldn't find a list anywhere (okay, I admit, I didn't really spend a lot of time looking because it's funnier to make my own list), I made my own list so I'd have a starting point to work with. After about five hours (okay, I admit, more like five minutes), I came up with the following possible super powers:

- Flight
- X-ray vision
- Superhuman strength
- Hands and fingers that turn into razor-sharp metal claws
- Fire-breathing
- Blue skin
- Muscles that help me run really fast, jump really high, and vacuum the first floor in record time

I had other things on the list—such as being a big rock or looking really cool wearing a long trenchcoat loaded with semiautomatic weapons—but I took those off the list early on. I already had more things on there than I knew what to do with. And, once I looked at the final entries, I realized just how pathetic a superhero I'd be. I didn't really want any of those powers, even if they were free.

Let's just dive right into it then:

Flight: I don't want to be able to fly for so many reasons it's not funny, and "not funny" isn't a good situation to be in when you're writing a humor book. But, the most obvious reason, besides the fact that I'm phobic about flying even in a device designed by brilliant engineers, is that I spent this summer watching various birds raise their young in various nests attached to various parts of my house. Learning to fly is not an easy task. Making that initial leap out of the nest requires intestinal fortitude that I do not possess. I can't even jump into a swimming pool if the water is below body temperature. I hem, I haw, I dip my toe in the water, and it takes me at least two hours to get myself into the water up to my knees. Getting the swimsuit wet requires a level of commitment higher than accepting a Mormon marriage proposal. Jumping off a building and flying? Yeah, I don't think so.

Besides, driving on the parkway at rush hour is enough travel excitement for me. Flying in the air means no guard rails, no left-turn-only lanes ... just open space in every direction. Unless I'd come equipped with a lot of rearview mirrors—well, mirrors *everywhere,* really—I don't want any part of that fiasco.

X-ray vision: The second power on the list is X-ray vision. You know, I barely tolerate seeing myself naked. And I see my husband naked because I think that's required by law. But anybody else? No, thank you. I've been on cruises where women twice my size wear swimsuits half the size of mine, and that's bad enough. The men are worse. Unless the X-ray vision came with parental controls on it to let in only certain images—like, say, Nathan Fillion or Johnny Depp—I'm not interested. Try to sell me some magazines I don't want or get me to become a Jehovah's Witness instead. You'll have better luck.

Superhuman strength: I don't want superhuman strength either, although at first this seemed like it had some possibilities. But, the more I thought about the fallout of having superhuman strength, the more I knew it'd have to be crossed off the list too. If I had that kind of power, my life would be total chaos. Besides, what would Wayne have left to make him feel needed? After all, I'd be able to open my own pickle jars. I could carry that new bookcase up the stairs without a furniture dolly. Plus, friends would start asking me to help them move. Friend with pianos or billiard tables. Or both.

And if I could lift anything—no matter how much it weighed—well, Wayne would start asking for piggyback rides. ("You going upstairs? Here, bend down.")

That's not a pretty sight. Not in my mind, anyway.

I have enough jobs to do without adding "human fork lift" to my list of daily tasks.

Hands and fingers that turn into razor-sharp claws: I admit, I only came up with this one because I remembered that one of the X-Men has this ailment. Yes, *ailment.* Who would want this super power? It's just Edward Scissorhands with a little more self-control, and a better complexion. Not very attractive, if you ask me (which you didn't). Can you imagine having those long, sharp metal claws sticking out of all your fingers? The only good thing is that you could slice a loaf of bread from across the kitchen without having to go get it first.

Beyond the usefulness of sporting a built-in kitchen utensil, all I see is annoyance. That, and probably being charged a lot more for a manicure. And the tip for that would have a lot more than twenty percent, wouldn't it? And, how do you brush your teeth with those claw things? And don't get me started on using the bathroom. This is probably why Wolverine has those ridiculous sideburns: He can't shave properly with those things! (Actually, if he was smart, he'd literally shave ***with*** those things. Might save him some money on razor blades.)

Let's move this super power list right along before somebody falls asleep. Namely, me.

Fire-breathing: I'm totally uninterested in being able to breathe fire, except when the barbecue grill runs out of propane or when my daughter and I are camping (again) in the rain (again) and we can't seem to get a campfire going. Or when I finally get on *Survivor*. But those three situations added together don't amount to enough momentum to get me to want to breathe fire.

Blue skin: Really? Why do some superheroes have blue skin? (I can think of two offhand who do, although I don't recall either of their names and I refuse to Google "blue-skinned superhero" while I'm sitting here at the Panera Bread.) Is blue skin less prone to sunburn? Goes better with certain types of hair? Keeps you cooler in summer? Doesn't clash with jeans the way chartreuse skin might? At least it would make those skin-tone product salespeople happy: "I'm pretty sure you're a Winter."

Muscles that help me run faster: I think the only item on my admittedly biased and incomplete list of super powers that even remotely piqued my curiosity was the last one: having muscles that enabled me to run faster, climb better, jump higher—all those exciting things I see people do in action movies. But I wouldn't want the muscles just so I could do what they do in action movies. Good grief, no. Jumping higher means overcoming a fear of heights first. Running faster means Wayne will ask me to save on gas by jogging to go shopping, which gives new meaning to the casual phrase, "Honey, I'm running to the store."

No, the only reason I'd want muscles like that—well, besides the fact that I'd probably have a slightly better physique—is so that I could climb the stairs with a laundry basket and not feel as if I'd just won the Tour de France without the help of performance-enhancing drugs.

Now *that* would make me feel like enough of a superhero to get me through the day. *Up, up, and away!*

That One Big Thing

So, I sit here with a stack of errands and miscellaneous to-do items that could stretch from here to West Mifflin if I let it. They're all things that need to be done eventually: doing a load of laundry, cleaning the upstairs bathroom, picking up some groceries, finishing the corrections on a book I'm typesetting (for someone else—not my book), unpacking more boxes (just so I can find my favorite pair of shoes, the digital thermometer, and a missing purple pillowcase ... and no, those three aren't related), watching back episodes of *Dark Shadows*.... You know, the stuff that makes up any normal person's day.

And yet, with so many of my heavy-commitment

events now gone for the year, I know it's time to dash through these mundane tasks and start carving out the writing time ... and guarding it. I've become convinced that I can no longer feel guilty about spending time each day writing, just because I like it a little too much. Perhaps I like it for a reason. Perhaps I like writing because it is my gift and I should be writing. Perhaps (and run with me yet one more step, but watch out for that twig or you'll trip) it would actually be wrong to engage only in everyday tasks and therefore neglect the one unique thing I may have been put here to do.

Yeah, I know: What's a humor writer doing sounding like there's some great force of destiny pushing her to write about her lawn mower, her waterbed, her adorably strange husband, and several bats who've gotten loose in her house this summer?

But honestly, work with me on this one. Long before I was a wife or a mother, I wanted to be a writer. I was eleven when it really hit me. By then I already owned a typewriter. (And what kind of ten-year-old asks for a typewriter for her birthday except one who is going to be a writer or a kidnapper?) Now I just needed the momentum.

I wrote a lot through my teen years, and then suddenly stopped when I got married a tad too young and had to face The Real World of putting food on the table, raising children on the world's smallest income, and shoving my needs and dreams to the back burner ... heck, shoving them entirely off the stove and onto the floor. (And yes, then I'd clean up the mess.)

So, if I sit around now, in my early fifties—having lived several lifetimes of experience, pain, anguish, and joy—and I choose to spend too much of my time keeping up with things that can essentially manage themselves with a lot less effort than I give them (*work smarter, Linda, not harder*), then I am wasting the time God's given me. I'm procrastinating on the One Big Thing I was put here to do—because I'm pretty sure it wasn't washing my husband's dirty socks or cleaning the vacuum cleaner filter for the umpteenth time, even though those things fulfill my soul every time I do them. And quit laughing.

Jesus' parable of the talents has been poking at me lately, and I really hate being poked. Especially by Jesus, because He's really good at everything. Being poked hurts, and I bruise easily.

So, now that my personal and professional schedules have both eased to the point where I can rearrange my priorities each day, it's time to buckle down, get some books out there, and take the world by storm. (Well, if not by storm, then at least a really nasty breeze and some drizzle.)

Who's with me?

Vying for Attention

It is an understatement to say that my husband, Wayne, is quiet. One night a thief broke into his truck (while it was parked against the house), stealing his laptop, his cell phone, his passport, and a bunch of other expensive, not-fun-to-lose items, and breaking his truck window to do it. Quiet Wayne called me on the phone and said simply (and quietly), "Just F.Y.I. There's been an incident at the house."

An incident? It sounded like I was being interviewed by a state trooper or the local sheriff for crimes as yet unnamed. Having the lawn mower run out of gas in the middle of mowing the lawn is an incident. This was a catastrophe. And, even after that, it took me a while to get the whole story out of him.

That's just his way, and most of the time I like that about him. No incessant chattering just to hear his own voice (like some people I know who write humor books). I especially love it when I ask him that all-important daily question: "How was work today, dear?" He'll launch into a story about the latest shenanigans at the plant (and really, what isn't fun about any story involving shenanigans at a nuclear power plant?), and I have to egg him on by asking impeccably timed questions that prove I'm paying attention to his story and not replaying that last episode of *Fringe* in my mind.

We'd gotten really good at the cat-and-mouse game of Twenty Questions (and Ten Answers), and then my brother-in-law Ed came to stay with us for a while. So now there were two semi-interested people asking Wayne twice as many questions as his introverted brain could handle. Most of the time we asked our questions at the same time, and if the questions had been at all related, poor Wayne could probably have handled them better. But I have a theoretical brain, and Ed has a mechanical brain—both of us asking Wayne's math brain to tell us how work was today, dear. (Well, Ed would leave off the "dear" part at the end. I hope.)

This interrogation exercise is the most fun when Wayne has been working the overnight shift on a 72-hour work week. By about Thursday, Wayne's coasting on sleep-fumes, nodding off at his computer mid-morning before collapsing into bed at high noon, only to hear the alarm go off at five P.M. so he can start it all over again. So, when Ed and I accost him upon his return in the morning, we have very different approaches to grilling the poor guy about his exciting twelve-hour overnight shift at the nation's first nuclear power plant. As a writer, I ask questions that will get Wayne to tell a story with a beginning, middle, and end. Ed, the brick mason and self-made mechanic, on the other hand, asks questions designed to reduce the nuke plant to a big ol' monster truck. A typical morning conversation with Nocturnal Nuke Boy goes something like this:

Me: So, how was work last night, dear?

Wayne: Wonderful.

Me: Really?

Wayne: *(says nothing, continues to download apps to his phone while nodding off in his 9 A.M. beer)*

Me: Did anything exciting happen?

Wayne: Well, somebody broke a crane.

Me: Ooh, did he get in trouble? Will he get fired? Will they deduct it from his pay?

Ed: *What kind of crane was it?*

Wayne: Big-ass crane. And we need it so we can keep the outage on schedule.

Me: Wow, does that mean the bosses are going to throw a hissy fit again?

Ed: *Where do they order parts for something like that? Online?*

Wayne: Westinghouse has to bring them in. We'll have to wait till the parts get here.

Me: Does this affect your department at all, or just the operators? Will you have to work on your off-day this week?

Ed: *The transmission in my truck is shot. I wonder if anyone working that crane would know how to –*

Wayne: *(changing the subject, even though we haven't really settled on a subject yet)* Looks like we're all getting upgraded to first-class for the rest of the outage.

Me: Oh good! So you guys won't have to file a grievance after all. I bet everybody is happy.

Ed: *Hey, that big thing by the road on the way into the plant.... Is that one of the turbines?*

Wayne: Yup.

Me: I've seen that thing. It scares me a little bit. I mean, I've seen *China Syndrome.*

Wayne: *China Syndrome* is ridiculous fiction. None of that stuff would happen in ... *zzzzzzzz ... (nods off in his beer, his nose hitting the foam and waking him up again)* Whuh? What time is it?

Ed: *Are the spent fuel pools around there anywhere? How do they encase that stuff properly so it doesn't leak?*

Me: (sighing) Wake up, Wayne. It's noon. Time for your nap.

Ed: *Can I change the battery in his truck while he's sleeping?*

Writers, Start Your Platens!

It says something about the state of our society when seven people can sit in the back room of a coffee shop and write ... and attract the stares of the other patrons and even the attention of the local newspaper. The seven of us are all writing feverishly and yet we're making more noise than most of the patrons in the main room combined. How can this be, you ask, if the writers aren't talking but are only writing their brains out?

Well, dear reader, I am writing this from The Great American Type-In at Cafe Kolache in Beaver, Pa. Yes, we're typing ... but we're typing on typewriters. Not just any typewriters, either. There is no electricity required for this type-in. We're sitting here using *manual* typewriters.

The strange part is all the prep work we had to do to get to this point. Hugh can't figure out how to release the carriage on his typewriter, and there are cries of "Release the Carriage!" from all corners of the room. Three writers hover around the Olympia typewriter, pushing every piece of metal sticking out of the thing, trying to get the platen to move. The victory shouts when the thing finally sails off to one side are deafening. But not as deafening as the noise coming from the other six keyboards.

Someone else tries to find the "on" button on hers. (Okay, that was me.) Turns out a manual typewriter doesn't have an "on" button. How very retro.

Shouts emanate from the gallery once we start the typing proper.

"Where is my apostrophe key?"

"Why isn't there a 'one' key?"

"What is this key that says 'MAR REL' on it?"

"No exclamation point! No exclamation point!" (It's an apostrophe and then a period after you hit the backspace key. And yes, I had to actually do that to get those exclamation points.)

My spacebar (which is not to be confused with the space bar in the first *Star Wars* movie) keeps giving up on me, and some of my words run together with no spaces before I catch the problem and physically pull the entire key set back into place. I discover early on that my old Royalite doesn't even have a tab key, and I must resort to the old method of manually spacing five counts on the spacebar to make a simulated tab. The problem, of course, is that the aforementioned space-bar doesn't always work, and so I end up with no tab/indent at all ... and after all that hard work, too.

Most of us have now been reduced to using three or four fingers since these blasted things have such sticky, difficult keys that we need some real "oomph" behind our typing to get the letters to show up on the page. And don't get me started on those sticky keys. I spent too much time last night prepping the keys with a few dozen Q-Tips and some rubbing alcohol ... and the question mark key is still sticking.

As a proofreader, I find this entire exercise vexing to the point of tears. I am making typos so fast I feel I will faint from the carnage. They'll have to cart me off weeping and gnashing my teeth by the time we're done here. I just checked the clock and it has taken me over an hour to type this much. Amazing how much my typing productivity plummets when I have to pound the keys.

That last paragraph has taken me twenty minutes to type, but this time it isn't the typewriter's fault. Hugh and Val have launched into a recreation of the last scene of *It's a Wonderful Life*, complete with all the characters' voices. We all feel the need to stop and listen and encourage them (not that either one of them needs encouragement) ... if only to give our tired index fingers a rest.

I have tried not to mention Val's typewriter because, well, it might embarrass him. You see, he brought this bright red plastic thing—well, it looks plastic, but it might actually have some metal on it—and I swear I saw a Fisher Price logo and an emblem of the Cookie Monster on the side. And that end-of-line bell sounds suspiciously like the Good Humor truck. But hey, it doesn't have a cord or a battery, so it's all good. Even if it does look more like a prehistoric Speak 'n Spell.

Nate's contraption (another Royal) has a button that says "Magic Column" on it. I begin to wonder if we should allow typewriters that have magic keys on them. Heck, I don't even have a tab key, let alone a magic key. I sense a growing hierarchy of typewriters in the room. I hadn't expected to experience typewriter envy, but I think some of us are ogling Roe's old Remington Rand. I know I am. Not so much Val's plastic Radio Flyer typewriter. Well, no, okay, that one too.

I sit here wondering how prolific writers of old ever churned out all those pages when it feels like a gym workout to get twelve words down at any respectable rate of speed. And now, having brought my productivity down to a mere two fingers, I find I have to look at the keys to make sure I hit the right ones at least ten percent of the time.

But I'm also starting to see the sheets of finished paper coming off the platens, being placed lovingly on the table around me. All facedown, of course, because we're all trying to hide the rampant typos spilling off every page. Well, okay, every line, really. None of us brought any Wite Out, and even I occasionally long for a spell checker. We have a ten-minute discussion on how to spell "bizarro," followed by another on how to spell "commode." Both questions come from the same person—okay, it was Val—so we all begin to wonder just what he's writing over there. Then we realize that no, we probably don't want to know.

Every so often, patrons from the main room drink enough coffee to brave wandering back here where the cacophony is erupting. They tentatively ask the question everyone else is thinking but is too frightened to ask us (since we all look like idiots back here and nobody wants to challenge the inner logic of an idiot on a mission): "What are you guys doing back here?" ... followed by a stunned utterance of, "Are those *typewriters*?"

Then they see seven of these things sitting on the long table, and their jaws drop. We look like the sad rejects of a small town news room, and Val's fedora with the handwritten "PRESS" pass bears this out. Not to mention Hugh's bowler hat, which I just mentioned.

And, like any cultural oddity, any societal deformity, we are eventually left alone again and ignored. Nothing to see here, people, nothing to see here. Move along....

Hugh's ribbon has now come to an end and has decided not to behave properly. It's supposed to reverse course on its own but it has abdicated this responsibility. It takes Hugh two minutes to figure out how to open the typewriter up to even get to the ribbon, and then he and Rachel take another ten minutes to figure out how to turn the ribbon around. They sound like car mechanics over there, and now Hugh has come back with a flashlight to look under the hood.

Another five minutes and they have the old ribbon out and have turned it around. There is a strange sense of pride when you get one of these beasts to submit. It's one thing to work out a software glitch with a Windows update ... but it is not as satisfying as getting one of these mechanical monsters to type that stray "e" that has been sticking on you for the first hour of typing.

Our time is through and we're wrapping things up now, after two hours of clicking and clacking (and bemoaning the fact that there was no whiskey in our coffee). I realize that, if we had been typing on laptops and tablets and netbooks, we wouldn't have heard nearly as many cries of "Ouch!" ... which came from those of us who got our fingers caught under the keys, where little keyboard monsters hide and nip at our fingertips. We'd have gotten more words written—properly spelled words, properly spaced words, words that would be readable once we got home—but they wouldn't have been **better** words. Just prettier words.

These words, *our* words, came with copious amounts of literal blood, sweat and tears today.

We *will* meet again, and we *will* conquer these machines. And, next time, like the fabled writers of old, there *will* be whiskey in our coffee.

Otherwise, most of us won't show up.

Things I Learned from Barnabas Collins

As part of my neverending quest to find ways to procrastinate on my writing, I'm knee-deep in old episodes of the 1960s gothic soap opera, *Dark Shadows*. I'm on episode 448 out of more than 1,200 episodes. I'm trying not to calculate just how much time I'll spend watching this entire show (*let's see, 21 minutes per episode times 1,245 ... divided by 60 minutes ... equals ... oh geez, I'm doomed ...*). But I know it's a boatload of time.

I console myself by saying that at least I put it on in the background while I'm working (or writing circular blog posts about it instead of writing). Sometimes that consolation is so thin I can see right through it, but today I decided to dig deeper (yes, I know—*graves, cof-*

fins, digging, ha ha ... Happy Halloween!), trying to find something of value in the ridiculous, inordinate, disturbing, amazing amount of time I'll be spending with this television series.

And, miracle of miracles, I found something!

Two-hundred-year-old vampire Barnabas Collins is played by the scrumptious Jonathan Frid. Frid isn't really known for anything else, but he's left an amazing legacy with this single part—in a poorly made, haphazardly shot soap opera whose recent revitalization through Netflix and DVDs is all the more extraordinary because other soap operas from that time period are all lost, the tapes having been erased or reused as was common for the time.

And because of the insanely tight production schedules of daily episodes going on for years, minor errors in production had to be overlooked. Then again, most of us today would likely define "minor errors" differently than producer Dan Curtis did at the time.

Most of the fun of watching *Dark Shadows* is waiting for the constant slips by the crew, and we needn't wait long: Boom microphones dangle onscreen from over the heads of the actors. Shadows of the cameraman and equipment loom large in every scene (which is probably where they got the name for the show). Flying rubber bats on strings attached to poles look pretty silly—especially when the strings and poles show up too, as if a stage hand is fishing for winged mammals on the set.

And then there is the house fly walking around on Frid's forehead for an entire scene ...

… and Frid never misses a line.

Oh, I do love that man.

All these glitches, goofs, and bloopers make an otherwise silly, campy show a glorious treasure to behold. And it makes me feel a little less guilty for spending so much time with Mr. Frid and his minions. There are lessons to learn and wisdom to be shared.

So, what life lessons has Barnabas Collins taught me? What redeemable qualities can the strange-looking vampire with the slicked-down hair and the omnipresent onyx ring have for someone like me?

I keep coming back to that fly on Frid's forehead. Frid not only doesn't acknowledge it, he stays in character. He goes on with his lines. While crew members are likely just off camera (for a change), giggling like schoolgirls, Frid remains his professional actor-self.

He stays on point. He doesn't waver. He knows there is a lot at stake here (*stake, ha ha ha …*). He knows they won't have time or tape to go back and redo the episode now. He also knows there isn't any CGI to cover up the fly in post-production. Well, he doesn't actually *know* about CGI, but you know what I mean.

Mr. Frid teaches me that I must keep moving forward, keep doing my duty—ignoring all flies on the forehead of life. Seems an easy, obvious lesson to some. But I too easily get sidetracked and lose my focus, swatting at imaginary flies that drive me batty (*batty, ha ha ha …*).

The fact that Frid can ignore real flies on his real forehead—while the whole world watches—is inspiring in its own way. If he can ignore such real vexations against all odds (and some of it is pretty odd!), then how much more can I ignore every pain in the neck (*pain in the neck, ha ha ha...*) that threatens to keep me away from my appointed tasks?

Thank you, Mr. Frid. The production values of your show may suck (*suck, ha ha ha ...*). Your character may suck. But you, sir, do not. You're bloody brilliant (*blo – never mind*).

Happy Halloween, Mr. Frid. You're sorely missed.

All Shall Be Well, and All Shall Be Well, and All Manner of ... Well, Now I'm Just Repeating Myself

I do some things the same way every time I do them. And, unlike the definition of insanity, I *do* expect the same result every time. That must be why I do it the same way: to get the same result. This does not mean I am not prone to bouts of insanity. It just means you'll have to use a different definition to include me.

I'm as much a creature of habit as anyone else, perhaps more so. The problem is, I picked some really boneheaded habits to be a creature of. Remember, these are things I have been doing repeatedly, for years, knowing full well what the results will be. That's probably just another definition of insanity.

Yes, I admit these are all stupid:

• I put ice cubes in a drink that's already cold from the fridge, even when I'm going to gulp it down in the next two minutes. Then I throw the ice cubes into the sink to die.

• I won't wear my house slippers into the dirty basement (I'll slide into a pair of old clogs instead), but I'll traipse out onto the dirty front porch to get the mail in those slippers. It's not like I vacuum the porch...

• I can go a month without dusting the living room, but I'll straighten all the throw pillows on the couch every time I walk by all day long, usually while mumbling about how careless some people are about such things.

• I keep in my office—set up and ready to use at a moment's notice—a laptop computer, two desktop computers, a typewriter, three Alphasmarts, two printers, and enough paper and pens to fill a small pickup truck ... and then I'll complain that I have nowhere to do my writing.

• I tell myself that, if I grade three student papers a day, I won't suffer trying to get them all in by the Tuesday midnight deadline each week ... but every time Monday rolls around I haven't touched any of them yet, and I spend the day putzing on Facebook and running errands to buy just the right lampshade, which means I spend Tuesday chained to my desk hearing the clock tick.

- **I eat low-carb and jog** up and down the huge staircases here, proud of myself for keeping my diabetes in check with simple changes instead of drugs or insulin... and then I stand too long at the checkout line in the grocery store and come home with a bag of Combos, which I eat all at once that same day.

- **I start the day** intending to finish writing that book soon, and then I find everything else on my mental to-do list (since I don't dare actually write this stuff down) *far* more fascinating and fulfilling than writing. This includes, but is not limited to, washing smelly laundry, cleaning the bathroom grout around the toilet, mowing the lawn, and discussing politics with a stark raving lunatic.*

And I could go on forever, but I won't because that lampshade still isn't quite right.

Running the risk of confusing myself, I hope to start shaking up my routine a little bit in order to fool myself out of some of these vexing habits. Maybe I'll give the Combos to a friend. Maybe I won't walk by the typewriter, the laptop, and the Alphasmart as if I

---

*I may or may not be referring to specific relatives.

don't even recognize them. Maybe I will log off Facebook and mark up a few student papers ... on a Thursday. Maybe I'll dust the whole first floor just because I can....

Okay, now I *know* I've gone too far. I've crossed the line into insanity. And the least you could do is look surprised.

In Which I Discuss My Brand

There's so much talk out there these days for authors to have a brand. At first I thought that sounded painful—I mean, I've seen enough westerns to know that branding involves hot spiky things and lots of mooing—but then I realized that it didn't mean a physical brand. But I'm still convinced it would involve a lot of pain and probably some mooing.

So, I learned the writer jargon-of-the-day and put the word "platform" on the back burner for now, despite the fact that I was convinced that standing on an author platform might at least make me a little taller and easier to see.

I'm always one step behind the changing lingo

of being a writer. It's bad enough that my work as a proofreader means buying new dictionaries like some people buy new iPhones. But somehow this author lingo never makes it into my new dictionaries fast enough for me to keep up with it. So I have to learn new words and catch phrases just like the little people do.

And I don't like it. I mean, I don't mind learning that "Google" is now a verb or that "anymore" is now one word or that the serial comma is a source of small civil war skirmishes in twenty-seven states, but that's because I get paid to learn that stuff. It seems a bit annoying at times to realize that "Ground Zero" means something entirely different now than it did when "Weird Al" Yankovic wrote his Christmas classic, "Christmas at Ground Zero," but I've learned to roll with those punches because it goes with the territory of being a good proofreader.

Somehow, though, I feel a smidge of personal offense that the powers that be (and who *be* they, exactly, and are they elected officials we can impeach?) have secret meetings every year or so to change the current word for ... well ... for "brand" or "platform" or whatever it was before "brand" and "platform." Just when I get used to the idea of needing a platform, I discover I'm too late and I need to ditch the platform and have a brand instead. And yet, just as the word "brand" starts to fade to be replaced with something else (within about six months, if I've done my math correctly), I'll realize that I didn't really get the hang of that either.

Until then, I suppose, I'll just have to be myself: a

wife, mother, and mostly family-friendly humor writer from western Pennsylvania who yearns to be the next big thing on the bestseller lists. There can't be more than one of me, can there? A benevolent God wouldn't allow it.

Waterbeds and the Elderly

Going into a second marriage in my late thirties was a wholly different experience than going into my first one at age twenty.

Merging two full-fledged households this time around meant a lot of picking and choosing: Do we use my portable dishwasher or his? Are his butt-ugly curtains going to stay on those windows, or can I surreptitiously switch them out for cute mini-blinds and valances and swags one day while he's working late? How many months will it take him to notice I've done this?

Do we have to endure his sectional sofa from the '80s just because it's still in good shape—well, since most of it is still in good shape? Why is that gargantuan electric organ still in the living room when it hasn't worked since 1983, making it little more than an annoyingly huge end table?

I answered most of these questions differently than Wayne did, and I massaged his opinion over to my way of thinking in nearly every single instance.

Except one.

We're still sleeping on the king-sized waterbed that has been in his possession since the disco era.

It's got this big round mirror on the headboard, and I always feel as if we are one mustache and ponytail away from making our own porn movie. And, just for the record, I never liked disco.

But, when Wayne and I got married, I moved my four children and me into his house, and apparently the waterbed had seniority. Plus, I brought into the marriage only a full-sized bed with a cheap mattress. There was no way we were going to start camping out on that thing. So, the waterbed won by default. I simply bought stock in Dramamine instead of arguing.

It's been nearly fourteen years since then, and we're still in that same waterbed.* Same rubber mattress. Same original mattress. Surely we are tempting fate with a mattress older than our children—several of whom are already married.

We've added more water to that antique mattress approximately once a year, which perplexes me. Where

*Well, not this very *minute*...

is that water going? If this is an airtight mattress—and let's face it, it has to be—how is any of the water evaporating? And how is enough of it evaporating that we can feel a difference at least once a year and have to add more water? (And before you ask, yes, with a garden hose… attached to the bathroom sink... and then with a few drops of bleach.)

We moved into a new house this past June—the first time that bed had been emptied and moved in about a quarter-century—and I had a brief, exciting thought that perhaps now we could start from scratch and rethink the waterbed idea. But Wayne's blank stare when I suggested a different bed spoke volumes. Volumes like, "What do you mean, get rid of my waterbed? Them's fightin' words."

People who buy waterbeds are like Apple fanboys. There's just no reasoning with them, no matter how much more logical it is to get a Sleep Number bed I can get in and out of easily or to get an inexpensive Windows computer with all that cheap software. I tried luring him into the Sleep Number bed idea because it comes with a remote control. What man can resist another remote control?

Apparently I married the one man who can.

I have tried to think of ways to get rid of this blasted waterbed without incurring the Wrath of Wayne (which has not been unleashed since the infamous Beer Distributor Strike of 2004). I thought perhaps an accidental, inadvertent, semi-planned puncture in the mattress would create enough of a setback for Wayne to rethink his loyalties, but the water damage alone would keep me from enacting this plan. Guess who would end up cleaning up the mess?

Plus, I doubt our homeowner's insurance covers flooding ... especially intentional flooding by waterbed.

So, to keep myself sane (knowing sanity is in the eye of the beholder), I've come up with some fun ideas for enjoying the waterbed without fear, anxiety, or motion sickness. If you're stuck with a waterbed, you can:

1. Buy a clear mattress and turn it into a koi pond. Then, time how long it takes to get to sleep with a bunch of big bulgy-eyed fish staring at you.

2. Install buoys along the middle and create swim lanes. Practice for the 2016 Olympics. After all, somebody's gotta replace Michael Phelps.

3. Stock the mattress with trout every spring. Let local fishermen use the water refill spout in the bottom left corner of the mattress the way ice fishermen use the little round holes they cut in the ice. Charge admission.

4. Save on heating bills in the winter by letting the mattress freeze over, creating an indoor skating rink. Market rubber-soled ice skates to keep from ripping up the mattress with regular skates. Charge admission.

5. Declare midnight to 1 a.m. "Adult Swim" time, if you know what I mean. Charge admission.

Rejected Book Titles

I'm probably not going to use any of these titles, so feel free to share with any writer friends you have:

What Could Go Wrong? An Electrical Rewiring Book for Dyslexics

Kim Kardashian's A Brief History of Time

An Engineer's Guide to "Mary Poppins" and "West Side Story" (with lyrics)

Ventriloquism for Dummies

Teenagers I Have Successfully Taught to Drive, by Linda M. Au (a pamphlet)

The Kama Sutra Pop-Up Book for Evangelicals

Thanks for Nothing

As I travel through this wondrous world, I'm constantly being thanked for things. No, I don't mean being thanked by people I know for favors I've done or services I've rendered. And no, I don't mean being thanked by other people for shutting up and leaving them alone, although that happens often enough that I'm beginning to think twice about those extra self-esteem webinars I've been meaning to take.

What I mean is, being thanked by inanimate objects—mostly signs—that thank me in advance for things I haven't even done yet. And, most likely, things I now have no intention of doing, at least not after encountering the stupid sign.

"Thank you for not smoking."

Hey, no sweat. I won't smoke. I don't smoke anyway. Never have. Never will. Wasn't even thinking about it until you mentioned it as a potential attention-getter. Maybe I'll skip out to the local corner store and pick up a pack and light up right here in front of the sign just because you expressly asked me not to. Either way, I'm gratified to learn you're concerned about my health.

"Thank you for protecting our waterways."

I saw this sign near a river. I'm not quite sure what I was doing to protect the waterways simply by standing next to the sign, but apparently I had magically warded off would-be waterway-ruiners with my presence. I envisioned myself dressed like Gandalf, with a staff in one hand, saying to illegal fishermen, "You shall not pass!"

Here I was, a Dudley Do-Right of the water supply, guarding all I surveyed simply by scanning the horizon and looking imposing.

No need to thank me. It was my pleasure.

"Thank you for your patronage."

If this were on a receipt for a hefty donation to the city's arts council, I might find it gratifying. But it's on the cheap, generic plastic bag my local Chinese restaurant uses when I order takeout. Some people are patrons of the arts. I'm merely a patron of moo-shoo chicken and a couple of egg rolls.

"Thank you for your patience."

This sign is a dead giveaway that I'm going to be sitting here a while. I just stepped into Waiting Room Hell, and the doctor's in the back playing Tetris on his iPad, mumbling "One more level!" while I sit out here reading back issues of *People* magazine with Burt Reynolds on the cover and watching seventeen people who came in here after I did go back for their appointments.

No, doctor, thank *you* for your patients.

"Thank you for your order."

I see this one after clicking "Place My Order" on every site on the Intrawebs. I'm not fooled, though. They're not really thanking me for my order, and I never feel appreciated. I just feel relieved that the WiFi didn't cut out in the middle of my click and that the order actually went through. That's all this thank-you really means: "Thank you for your order. The Internet cooperated for five full seconds and your order is now off in our warehouse computer somewhere. As soon as the IT guy figures out what he did wrong setting up our ordering system in the first place, we might actually *see* your order and assemble it. That is, assuming something isn't on backorder. Which is entirely possible, since we had to order stuff from other vendors, and we got this nice screenshot after we ordered it all, thanking us for our order."

"Thank you for paying in advance."

This little gem shows up right inside the front door of doctors' offices and auto body shops and port authority buses and a few eating establishments where it's not clear whether I'm supposed to order up front like a fast-food place or sit down, eat, and wait for a check like a restaurant.

In all cases, it borders on rude, but because they're thanking me for something as soon as I step in the door, it takes me a few minutes to feel offended. Because if I'm in the doctor's office with the flu, feeling as if breakfast might reappear at any moment, I might not be in a hurry to find offense in that sign laser-printed on 20-lb. bond paper and taped to the wall. The only thing I'm doing in advance is vomiting or making a mental note not to come back here any time soon.

You're welcome.

Lint in My Pockets

I often have way too many strange thoughts during a typical day to keep track of. So, I write them down. Sometimes, though, they're not big enough thoughts to go out into the world all by themselves, so they need some company.

That's where essays like this one come from. These are stray thoughts that don't need an entire page to themselves. Kinda like finding a bunch of lint in your pants pocket: It feels like something important, until you pull it out into the light of day and look at it more closely. Then you just don't know what to do with it.

Here is some of the lint in the pockets of my mind, so to speak:

* **Men who can't play basketball** play wastebasketball instead.

* **What about the infrastructure, people?** All the road signs around here are missing so many letters I feel like I'm playing "Wheel of Fortune" while driving to the grocery store. Can I buy a vowel ... and a dozen eggs?

* **Toothpaste companies** all discriminate against people who don't like mint.

* **I love going to the movie theater,** but I don't know why. After all, I pay an obscene amount of money to sit next to strangers on cell phones and toddlers with head colds instead of watching a movie in my own home. Why? Just so other people can influence when I laugh?

* **It's 2013 as I write this.** Windows 8 has been out for a while now. Should I be concerned that the nuke plant where my husband works just upgaded all their computers ... to Vista?

* **Some nights I wake up** in a cold sweat from one of my worst nightmares: that they outlawed refrigerators made of metal and switched to plastic instead, rendering all my fridge magnets useless unless I want to break out the glue stick.

* **I know my diet is going badly** when road signs that say "Weight Limit 7 Tons" intimidate me.

* **What will God call us** when we get to heaven? Is it really going to be the names our parents gave us? Because some of our parents were drunk or otherwise entirely too random back then for us to be stuck with these names for eternity. And yet, if God started calling me "Sally" when I got to heaven, I'd probably inadvertently walk right by.

* **From the** Things I Won't Explain Further Department: No self-respecting woman likes those auto-flush toilets.

* **You know it's going to be a bad road trip** when you get off an exit for lunch and stop at a Burger King, only to be told their broiler is broken and they have "everything but the burgers." Because, yeah, I stopped here specifically for your salads ...

* **I'm not a conspiracy theorist,** but in my neighborhood there is a funeral home right next door to a nursing home. Note to my children: Please send me to any *other* nursing home when I am old.

* **This country has already become** way too germophobic, but I still think the next big marketing ploy will be antibacterial food.

* **One day my husband came home** from work at the nuclear power plant early. "They sent us home because the power went out." How does the electricity go out at the place that makes the electricity? And, should I be worried?

* **I saw one of those** teeny tiny "smart cars" going through the car wash. Are there discounts for smart cars? And why would you even bother to pay for a car wash when you can probably clean the entire outside of the car with a wet wipe and a Q-Tip?

* **There's a small neighborhood store** in Ohio called George's Party Pack and Hardware Store. They sell plastic cups and napkins ... and beer ... and power tools. I'm stunned that they think it's a good idea to sell power tools to the same person they're selling beer. Then again, I don't live in Ohio. There might be a cultural barrier I'm not aware of because I live twelve miles away in Pennsylvania. You know, the state where you can buy liquor only at government-sanctioned State Stores.

* **Where does the toilet water** on a cruise ship go when you flush? Are staterooms near that spot a little cheaper?

* **I don't need a shoe horn.** I need a sock horn.

* **I wonder if it's safe** to sleep in a waterbed during a thunderstorm.

Obsolutely!

Things I Remember Fondly That Are Obsolete Now

* **Phone books**

* **Fax machines**

* **Rolodex files**

* **Land lines** (which are beginning to sound vaguely nautical to the younger generation)

* **Disco**—and I remember it fondly precisely *because* it is obsolete

* **Roller skates**—you know, the kind with four wheels set in a pattern like the wheels of a car ... the kind I could actually skate with, without toppling over

* **Every car** I have ever owned up until now

* **Tape decks**—except the ones in every car I have ever owned up until now

* **My hairstyle**

* **Any piece** of technology five minutes after I buy it

* **Most of the clothing** in my closet, plus all of the clothing I'm going to buy within the next year

Why Mankind Is Above the Animals

* Dogs don't get the subtlety of puns.

* Cats can't grasp the meaning of birthday cake.

* Animals will never find a substitute for opposable thumbs.

* Humans appreciate the value of clothing, especially in cold weather or on uglier members of the species.

* Pets don't understand thunderstorms. They also confuse your leaving a room with your winking out of existence completely.

* Humans know they're going to die. We don't like it, but we understand it.

* Air-conditioning.

* We can put a man on the moon ... and a Starbucks on every corner.

Why Mankind Might Not Be Above the Animals

* Humans weren't smart enough to make any bank holidays or three-day weekends in August.

* We shovel snow instead of hibernating under it.

* We have politicians.

* Fat animals look cute. Fat humans, not so much ... with the possible exception of me in a really cute new outfit on a good hair day. But even then, let's face it, I'm no baby bunny.

* Justin Bieber and/or Honey Boo-Boo.

* We can put a Starbucks on every corner ... and we usually do.

Dante's Nine Circles of Showering

1st Circle: Winter. Working from home. Weather too awful for anyone to actually brave driving to the house to visit. Forget it, I'm not showering today.

2nd Circle: Winter. Snow flurries. Working from home but have a few errands to run. I can do all of them from drive-thru windows and don't have to get out of the car. If I can't skip showering entirely, I can at least get away with a five-minute hair-scrub and let the shampoo act like gravity-induced body wash.

3rd Circle: Still winter, but weather is merely chilly. To maximize days where I can get to my car without shoveling a foot of snow off the hood, I'll break down and run errands today—errands that involve getting out of the car and interacting with other human beings face to face. I'll have to shower properly, but maybe I can skimp on washing my hair and just wear a winter hat. I'll probably give in and brush my teeth and use deodorant. I hope everyone appreciates the extra effort. But I'm ***not*** shaving!

4th Circle: Spring. Technically speaking. I can get away with a sweater instead of a coat while I run errands, but the winter hat would look stupid so I'll have to shower and wash my hair. Unless I can find a baseball hat.

5th Circle: Really spring now. Ground thawed. Gardening has started. Time to wear capris but still too cool for sandals. Although I won't need to loofah my feet, I can't put off shaving any longer. I haven't shaved since sometime last November, so I will spend 20 minutes under the water and use up at least three razor blades. And yet, I shaved my legs only up to the knees because of the capris. Bleeding and swear words optional (but likely).

6th Circle: Late spring. Temperatures near 90 some days, with lingering frost warnings overnight. Since I can't always be a night owl, I have to go out in public during daylight. This now means shorts. Shorts now mean shaving up past my knees. There is weeping and gnashing of teeth. And more bleeding.

7th Circle: Early summer. Annual appointment with the dermatologist. Showering involves using two different types of dandruff shampoo, a light conditioner, and then a mild facial scrub that won't irritate and inflame my rosacea. Cleaning everything from the neck up takes approximately seventeen minutes, depending on whether or not I tilt my head wrong and get water in one of my ears. Plus, you know, the shaving everything from the neck down thing ...

8th Circle: Summer. On a cruise ship. We signed up for a snorkeling excursion in the Caribbean, so I have to shower, shave underarms and both legs up as high as the swimsuit skirt, all the while thanking God for the invention of swimsuits with little skirts, made for middle-aged women.

9th Circle: Season is irrelevant. Yearly routine appointment with gynecologist. This means I'll be in the shower for the next two hours shaving every square inch of skin. But I'm ***not*** waxing!

Linda Abhors a Vacuum

Every vacuum cleaner I've ever owned has rebelled as soon as I got into the habit of actually using it. Well, that's a bit of an exaggeration. I don't think I've ever been in the *habit* of using a vacuum cleaner. I've *inadvertently* used a vacuum cleaner on the same carpet more than once in the same month, and that's been my working definition of "habit" ever since.

What's not an exaggeration is their rude and unprovoked rebellion. They refuse to pick up that paper clip, or even that stray bit of paper, or especially that bread bag twist tie, and they make me run over the same spot on the rug twenty, thirty, sometimes forty times in a vain effort to prove to myself that machinery and technology have made my life easier than my grandmother's, even though she would have simply bent over and plucked the paper clip off the carpet with her fingers within the first ten seconds and been done with it. But I have made it a personal goal to get the stupid thing up without bending over or giving in. Showing weakness in the face of the enemy is bad. Letting the enemy see your fear is the beginning of the end.

Right now I own three upright vacuum cleaners. I bought the first one when the previous one bit the dust, so to speak. Actually, if it bit the dust, I wouldn't have had to buy the new one. When we moved into our new house, my mother upgraded her own vacuum cleaner and gave me her "old" one—which wasn't really old, of course. She just got tired of it. It was an exact replica of the one I already had, which was beginning to sound weary and unenthusiastic about the one job it was put on the planet to do. She told me now I wouldn't have to cart my single vacuum cleaner all the way up and down the grand staircase. I could now have a vacuum cleaner on each floor. And since it was a machine my mother had owned for only a few nanoseconds (and that she had cleaned thoroughly after every usage), I was glad to have a vacuum cleaner I was familiar with, that actually still worked properly.

But I had just replaced my own iffy first-floor vacuum cleaner with a newer, lighter vacuum cleaner with a lot more suction. Or so I thought. The belt broke and the filter clogged badly, and no amount of cleaning seemed to get its suction back. And of course, it had been orphaned by the company about three minutes after I bought it, so finding a new belt and filter turned into a scavenger hunt that looked like it was going to involve mainland China and cheap shipping that would take three months to get everything to me.

During the several months the dance of the three vacuum cleaners went on, I was hoisting each of them up and down both staircases, trying to remember which one actually still worked and which one was a mere shell of its former self. Naturally, any time I bothered to lug one of these cumbersome things up twenty steps, I'd see the other two at the bottom of the steps and knew I had again brought the wrong one upstairs. It'd be a compliment to them to say these other two vacuum cleaners sucked. They didn't suck. Not at all. That was the problem in a nutshell. And speaking of nutshells, they wouldn't pick up any of those either.

One time I chose a random vacuum and pitched it down the steps over the banister in a fit of wicked glee, shattering plastic, and flying dust bunnies that gave me more of a sense of domestic accomplishment than I had had in years. It wasn't until I looked more closely at the two remaining vacuums that I realized I had pitched the only good one. The one I could still get parts for. The one my mother had given me—the heirloom vacuum cleaner. I had become momentarily disoriented by the small bungee cord my dad had strapped onto the plastic foot pedal to keep it from falling off every time my mother had tried to turn it on. My brain had assumed that any vacuum cleaner jury-rigged with a bungee cord had to be the bad one. What I had failed to factor in was the fact that the thing needed the bungee cord because my mother the clean freak had worn out the on/off pedal by using it so often. If I had taken a moment to check the matching vacuum cleaner, I would have seen dust and cobwebs on the on/off pedal … a dead giveaway that it had been mine.

Lesson learned.

And actually, I was fibbing about throwing the good vacuum cleaner down the steps. That was just a really vivid nightmare I had a few weeks ago.

I am now left with one orphaned vacuum cleaner without spare parts (or working original ones), a first vacuum cleaner that sucks because it doesn't suck, and a third, gift vacuum cleaner that works, as long as it's on the right floor on the right day. My mother, in her well-intentioned effort to save me the hassle of toting a vacuum cleaner up and down the steps, has made me hoist three vacuum cleaners up and down the steps any time I even *think* about cleaning a floor in my house.

It's a good thing I so rarely think about cleaning a floor in my house, or I'd be exhausted.

Rebels Without a Cause

Teenagers go through a rebellious stage. This is an empirically verifiable fact. (If you know any empires, go ask them.) My own definition of rebellion came and left early. I had a single puff of a cigarette on a crowded drum & bugle corps bus when I was ten years old. Gagged and coughed and never did it again ... although I suspect my mother will finally find out about my pre-teen rebellion when she reads this book. After that day, I signed up for the Goody Two Shoes club. And I wasn't just a client; I was also the president.

Now I'm a mother of four grown children, so you'd naturally assume I'm an expert on what teen rebellion looks like, having been through it four times.

Yeah, well, not so much. Oh sure, each one of my kids *rebelled*—just not in a normal way. And because none of them would admit to any of this in court (they wouldn't even give a proper deposition or respond to the subpoenas), I won't use their real names.

Random Child #1: Sneaks out of the house by climbing onto the porch roof outside the bathroom window ... only to run around the block and come back, trying to convince us he was just passing by and was never in the house. Doesn't realize the idea is to sneak out and stay out.

Random Child #2: Edits the Wikipedia entry for "Gangsta Rap" by adding herself and her brother as world-famous rappers Mixmasta G-Munnie and MC J-Hunnie. It takes a month before someone catches the error and fixes it, proving once again why you should never rely solely on Wikipedia for source material.

Random Child #3: Tries to dye the lower half of her long hair bright purple by bleaching it, then applying purple hair dye. Asks mother's and father's permission first. Apparently doesn't understand the basic concept behind teenage rebellion. Asks advice when hair turns pink after two washings. Mother draws a blank but tells her the pink looks lovely.

Random Child #4: Decides emphatically not to go to college. Anywhere. Ever. Mother protests. Child has his own stock portfolio by the age of twenty and sells a single Web site he designed for $14,000. Mother stops protesting and asks if she can borrow a couple hundred bucks till the weekend.

Signs of the Times

I get bored when I'm driving routinely down the same old roads. Since I'm not allowed to text while I drive and since drinking a few margaritas while behind the wheel is apparently frowned upon by decent society, I have to find something else to keep my brain occupied. You know, besides paying attention to the innocent lives around me in other cars.

So, instead of focusing my attention on the road in front of me, I read all the signs along the way. They're obviously put there so I'll read them, so in a way it would be a great disservice to the kind folks who made them if I ignored them. Right?

Some of the things I found, though, were scarier

than the thought of me driving a car and texting while violating the open container laws of Pennsylvania.

"Road Work 1 Mile." This sign doesn't help anybody prepare for whatever lies ahead in one mile. What's going to happen in one mile? Will a lane be closed? Will the shoulder disappear? (Notice that I didn't ask whether anyone will actually be working. This is PennDOT we're talking about.)

Traffic Cones. Here in Pennsylvania the road crews take the time and trouble to pave over dead deer on the shoulder of the road, which takes more skill and finesse than you might think. Getting those painted white lines up over the belly lump is particularly tricky. In neighboring Ohio, though, they simply put up traffic cones around Roadkill Rudolph and leave it at that. Perhaps in December they'll hang some twinkle lights.

"Speed Enforced From Aircraft." This one has confused me ever since I saw it for the first time as a child. To this day I have no clue what it really means, but I keep picturing Cary Grant in a nice suit running down an open stretch of highway with a small plane buzzing him overhead. That's probably not what it means, though. For one thing, Cary Grant wasn't even in a car, let alone speeding.

Homemade Signs. On the way home from a big flea market in Ohio, I saw the following handmade sign on a lawn near the border with Pennsylvania: "Notary. Brown Eggs." Anything I could come up with to write here wouldn't be nearly as funny as letting you figure out something on your own. Enjoy.

"Toledo: 150 Miles." At some point in the history of mankind, Toledo became the center of the universe. When traveling on turnpikes and interstates from Pennsylvania heading west (or from any point farther west heading east), all signs giving you some indication of where you are on God's green earth include where you are in relation to Toledo. I've never actually been to Toledo, but it must be all kinds of awesome. Or, maybe, all kinds of scary. Either way, I picture a Tardis right in the middle of the downtown area.

"Prison Area. Do Not Pick Up Hitchhikers." Seriously? For one thing, this really doesn't say very much about the prison security, does it? Aren't they supposed to, well, keep those prisoners *inside* the prison and not let them hitchhike along the side of the road? For another thing, they should update the sign so it's a little clearer for the less intelligent drivers out there: "Prison Area. Do Not Pick Up Hitchhikers Wearing Orange Jumpsuits And/Or Shackles Or Brandishing Shivs."

Things That . . .

Things That I Found in Our New House:

* 8 pennies, 1 quarter (I'll put it toward the mortgage.)
* 1 superball eyeball
* 2 regular superballs
* 1 set of car keys (How did the previous owners ever leave without their car keys? Maybe they're still here.)
* 1 mystery key (to add to my collection of mystery keys from all the other places I've ever lived. It's about time to call the Smithsonian.)
* 2 old prescriptions, one of them for a dog (The two prescriptions were next to each other in a kitchen

cabinet. I have no idea what that means, but the dog probably didn't suffer from anxiety anymore and the owner finally licked that nasty flea problem.)

* 1 spider (Yes, just one. Fine with me. This isn't Noah's Ark, after all.)

Things That I Have Been Putting Off:

* Cleaning the refrigerator

* Cleaning just about anything else

* Running a marathon

* Running up the steps

* Running my mouth off (No, wait, I'm all caught up on that.)

* Performing open-heart surgery

* Performing "Pineapple Princess" on my ukulele

* Losing weight

* Losing my mind (Actually, I'm ahead of schedule on this one.)

Things That I Regret Killing:

* Stink bugs in my house (I'm afraid their friends and family will exact revenge by killing me in my sleep.)

* That squirrel I hit with my car a few years ago (But honestly, he ran right into the road and there was no shoulder for me to swerve onto. The nightmares, though ... oh, *the nightmares*...)

* My buzz

* That hitchhiker who ... never mind.

Things That I'd Like to Snipe on eBay:

* A winning Powerball ticket

* The entire contents of the Levenger catalog (with free shipping)

Things That My Husband Doesn't Notice:

* My new haircut, even if my legally blind friend at church complimented me on it a week earlier

* Our anniversary or my birthday or Valentine's Day or Christmas ... or Tuesday

* Whether I am at home when he gets home from work

* Whether I've been at home for the past week and a half

Things That I Forget:

* My driver's license number

* My bank account number

* My keys as I slam the locked car door shut

* All the really funny ideas I don't write down as soon as I think about them (which is obvious by the time you hit this point in the book)

Things That Make Me Sleepy:

* Over-the-counter sleep aids (Well, okay, that one's obvious.)

* Melatonin (Yes, all right, that one's obvious too.)

* A turkey dinner (especially if I have to cook it and clean up after it)

* A Big Gulp of Old Crow bourbon mixed with a shotglass of Caffeine-Free Diet Coke

* Doing housework

* Thinking about housework

* Thinking

* Episodes of narcolepsy

* Episodes of *Glee*

How Do I Love Thee? Let Me ~~Count~~ Calculate the Ways

When your husband is an engineer, you get used to strangely crafted declarations of love. After all, you've been chosen by a man who dreams of clearance sales at Harbor Freight Tools, and whose idea of a romantic getaway is a fun-filled weekend defragmenting all the computers. What did you expect, flowers and chocolates?

Wait, seriously? You expected flowers and chocolates? You'll learn. Oh yes, you'll learn.

When other men are taking their wives out to dinner at fancy restaurants for their anniversaries, your engineer husband takes you to McDonald's because he has a coupon and they have free WiFi now.

When other men take their wives on cruises, your engineer husband won't go back to Cozumel because he didn't like the look of that substandard electrical wiring on the telephone poles outside Señor Frog's right off the dock.

When other men buy their wives roses, your husband apologizes for no flowers this year because he's busy working on a hybrid rose that doesn't have any thorns and he lost the schematics he drew up on the cross-pollination of hybrid roses when they flew out of the flatbed of his truck on his way to Lowe's to buy potting soil for the hybrid roses.

Other men give their wives an occasional day off from household chores like cleaning and laundry, helping them by doing the vacuuming themselves. Your husband buys you a refurbished off-brand Roomba from eBay and wraps it in the color comics page from the Sunday paper because he doesn't have a clue where you keep the wrapping paper. Or the tape. And he brags about the free shipping he got because he also ordered another Shop Vac for the garage.

Some men treat their wives to coupons for complete spa days to pamper them. Your man hotwires the bathroom with fake "flickering" candles that work by remote control and then adds an electrical outlet in the medicine cabinet so you can put in an iPod dock filled with Michael Buble songs.

While most men take their wives in their arms and whisper sweet nothings in their ears, your engineer husband takes you in his arms and asks, "What do you weigh now?" so he can buy you a porch swing that will properly support your weight when he jury-rigs it to the beadboard ceiling of the front porch.

When normal husbands take their wives out to a movie and let them choose a chick flick or a date movie, your engineer husband buys a 65" SmartTV for the living room and pulls the shades so the two of you can watch the history of duct tape on the Discovery Channel together in the dark. He lets you make the popcorn.

A few husbands might get more romantic and take their wives to a drive-in movie for a little nostalgic making out in the car. Your engineer husband will take you to the drive-in but will then decide he doesn't like the clicking sound he's hearing from under the hood and will get out the ratchet set he keeps in the trunk and tinker with the engine for the first two-thirds of the movie, while you sit in the front seat staring at the raised car hood. He lets you buy the popcorn.

Other men get the air-conditioning units back in the windows by sometime around Memorial Day. Your engineer husband is busy calculating the amount of torque needed to use the two-inch wood screws instead of the inferior dry wall screws this year while installing the window unit using pieces of scrap lumber from last year's bathroom project. The air conditioning unit is safely tucked into the window and fully functional by sometime around Labor Day.

You see, it's always a tradeoff with an engineer husband. You have to put up with him carrying a Swiss Army knife and a tape measure on his keychain and wearing a pocket protector on vacation, but you also get a guy who knows how to wield a slide rule like Clint Eastwood wields a .357 Magnum. Seems to me it's a win-win for everybody. Except I still have no idea what a slide rule is for.

If Cars Could Talk

A few decades ago, a title like "If Cars Could Talk" would have conjured images of Kit from *Knight Rider*. A few more decades ago, it would have brought forth images of *My Mother the Car*. (If you've never heard of either of these TV shows, remember: This is why God invented Wikipedia and IMDb.)

But my 2010 Cobalt comes in a close second to those famous cars, considering it doesn't audibly talk to me (that you're aware of). It does, however, send me messages all the time while I'm driving:

* **Ice Possible.** When the outside temperature falls below 32° Fahrenheit, the dashboard reads: "Ice Pos-

sible." Oh yes, *now* I remember: Water *freezes* at 32°. It's like eighth grade science all over again. And I didn't really like it the first time back in 1974. But thanks for the warning.

* **Tire Pressure Low.** Don't get me wrong: I'm thrilled that I don't have to proactively check the pressure in my tires anymore (which implies I ever did it in the first place—honestly, does any decent woman check her tire pressure? "Let's see, I could check the pressure in my tires, or watch the latest episode of *Downton Abbey* ... tough call ..."). But, why does this car warning always come up the second I hit an on-ramp for the turnpike, where the exits are about thirty miles apart? That bicycle pump back home in the garage ain't gonna do me any good now.

* **Low Fuel.** What's with all the "low" warnings? Low temperatures, low air in the tires, low gas in the tank. Why must my car always be so negative? And why don't I carry a gas can in the trunk?

* **That steering wheel makes you look fat, and those shoes don't go with that dress.** Okay, now that's *really* low!

Gadget Geeks, Unite!

I like to think that my engineer husband and I have a few things in common, and that those common bonds brought us together back in 1999 when we fell in love and got married.

I also like to think that I look more like Sandra Bullock than Rosie O'Donnell, but hey, that ain't happening either, is it?

We do, though, both have a love for and fascination with electronic gadgets. Wayne likes to take out all the screws and pins, take them apart, upgrade them, rewire them, and tinker with them right out of the box. I like to, well, *use* them.

Okay, so maybe we see our beloved gadgets a little differently. Maybe I'm a little behind the times because

I use eBay to buy fifty-pound IBM Selectric typewriters that set off the seat belt sensor in the passenger seat when I take them in to be serviced.

Maybe I see a woman using her indoor vacuum cleaner outside on her sidewalk to suck up dirt, the long cord and an extension cord slithering its way back through the front door, and I say, "Why?" And maybe Wayne sees that same woman and says, "Why not?"

Maybe I think that calling an older television "portable" doesn't just mean putting a handle on it if it weighs over a hundred pounds and has a circumference the size of a small planet.

Maybe I don't call it progress when we move from a stack of paper towels in the public restroom to an automatic hand dryer that blows cold air over your hands so slowly you have to sign a lease to stay in the bathroom any longer. Maybe I prefer those newfangled hand dryers that move the hot air around so fast you can watch your skin move around on the back of your hand, almost as if you'd stuck your hand in a NASA G-force machine. Oh sure, the skin on your hand now flaps around like your grandmother's flabby biceps (or mine, let's face it), but at least your hands are dry.

It doesn't matter how I view other people's gadgets and how they use them, because I'll always cherish the matching laptops my husband and I share, the universal remote he got me for our last anniversary (even though he never lets me touch it), and the extra hard drive he installed for our DVR so I can record episodes of *Mad Men* for later (and let him watch *Duck Dynasty* now).

Love Me, Love My Car

For most of my adult life, I've owned used cars. Well, "used" is putting it mildly. "Manhandled" or "tortured" might be more accurate. Half the stuff on the car didn't work when I bought it, and after that point I got used to watching one feature and then another stop working ... until one day I'd start the car and the only thing that still worked was the handle for the back passenger window, but only if I had a pair of pliers handy. And maybe the AM radio worked. *Maybe*. Never the FM radio, though, and certainly not the driver's side front window. I mean, a girl couldn't get too greedy ...

I used to know that secret language of every used car owner. You know the one I mean: where you turn the key and the car doesn't start, so you begin to coo and purr at it, leaning your face ever so close to the steering wheel, whispering promises you never intend to keep: "C'mon, baby, start up for me and I'll change your oil. And none of that chintzy synthetic stuff, either. C'mon ..."

After ten more tries at starting the car, you're not quite desperate, but you're a bit unsettled and upset ... and late for work. You continue the promises, upping the ante a little with sworn decrees and signed affidavits that you'll never load your precious baby down with 50-pound bags of mulch in the back seat ever, ever again. But now you're not cooing or purring. You're promising through gritted teeth and trying to sound sincere.

Ah, but that 1989 Ford Escort with the front bumper covered in duct tape is onto you, isn't it? It knows you don't mean a word of it. So, it sputters and dies yet again, refusing to even come close to turning over. Now you're down to a faint clicking noise any time you turn the key. And a quick glance at your watch tells you that lunchtime at the office is almost over. And you regret yet again not having renewed your AAA membership with the free towing.

So now you're done with promises and have moved on to thinly veiled threats, immediately followed by threats not veiled at all, as well as shrieks for vengeance and a few ancient voodoo curses, all while pounding the steering wheel with both fists. The neighbors now think you're insane, but they probably thought that yesterday too, so why not go for it and give them the show they've been expecting since you first moved in?

Used car owners come in two flavors: eternal optimists and eternal pessimists. Most of us start out as the former, hopefully pushing the button for the air conditioning on the dashboard in July—a button that didn't work when we bought the car, didn't work yesterday, won't work tomorrow, and won't work even after Jesus comes back—and thinking that today, *yes, today,* the air conditioning will pump cool refreshing air into the car. Suddenly we believe a car can magically heal itself. Ah, stupidity springs eternal. And, of course, Freon springs out of the hoses if they're busted.

Either way, we're sweating out the rest of the summer on those long commutes stuck in traffic on the highway under the blazing sun. It's a good thing that handle on the back passenger window still works. Now, where are those pliers?

Stocking Up for the Zombie Apocalypse

Most of us are ready for the upcoming zombie apocalypse. We've watched all current episodes of *The Walking Dead*. We've got canned goods in our basements. We're seriously considering getting the ol' crossbow out of storage just in case they show up tomorrow. (They'd better not show up tomorrow, though. I'm way behind on the laundry.)

I like to be as well prepared as the next guy when it comes to doomsday scenarios. My daughter even coached me through my first attempt at a bug-out bag so I'd be ready for anything. (I did a good job with the military MREs and the first-aid kit, but she thought the portable DVD player with all four seasons of *Battlestar*

Galactica was kind of missing the point.) And I also figure we have enough blankets and propane and candles and camping gear and crank-handled weather radios to get us through the initial outbreak and panic periods.

But someone has got to tell my husband to just STOP already. He's an undiagnosed hoarder (it's a tricky diagnosis, but the stack of expired credit cards from the 1980s and the Betamax exercise tapes are a dead giveaway), and even if that zombie apocalypse *does* happen tomorrow (and really, I hope not, because I still have to get my hair cut), Wayne will be more than ready. The only sad part is that he's not doing it on purpose.

I thought Wayne bought the pickup truck with the extended cab a few years ago so he could invite friends or family to travel with him in his many jaunts to interesting places. Then I remembered that he doesn't go on any jaunts to interesting places, unless you count the construction auction in North Lima, Ohio ... which I don't.

Turns out he upgraded to the extended cab so he'd have room to store entire cases of ramen noodles and bottled water back there. The man stocks food in his truck the way grocery stores stock canned goods on their shelves, and yet if I want to eat a single French fry in the front seat, he shrieks like a little girl that he never lets anyone eat in his truck. I'm not sure how or why twelve thousand leftover straws, napkins, and packets of picante sauce from McDonald's got onto his dashboard, but I suppose he's got a likely story for that.

If the basic food supply weren't enough to make me want to camp out in his truck away from the zombies, then the hand tools, bungee cords, dollar-store LED mini-flashlights, Pop-Tarts, USB port adapters, concealed weapons, and cans of every sort of vehicle fluid imaginable would certainly make me consider it my home away from home. A few throw pillows and a cross-stitch sampler, and I'd move right in.

Heck, I've lived in apartments smaller than that truck. Not nearly as cluttered, but smaller.

I've asked him about the McDonald's straws more than once. I'll keep asking until I get an answer that makes sense. Most of those things have been on the dashboard so long that the paper has disintegrated and they'll need carbon dating to determine how long they've been there. We'll probably end up spending the zombie apocalypse sharing the truck with Allan Grant and Louis Leakey.

We've got the rest of the zombie apocalypse beat, though. With Wayne's vast collection of AK-47 ammunition, Bowie knives, Sam Adams beer, and bottle openers, we're all set. Those zombies are definitely going to steer clear of the Parker household if they know what's good for them. Then again, so will most of the neighbors. And most of our kids.

Well, maybe we'll add more beer.

And drink it with the straws.

Follow the Bouncing Ball

Not all kids can boast about having cool parents. Certainly, my own kids can't. (I once tried convincing them I was cool by seeing Nine Inch Nails live in concert, but I found myself turning to all the teenagers smoking pot around me and saying, "Does your mother know you do that?" That immediately negates all the cool points. That, and the cheap Birkenstock knockoffs and semi-mullet haircut. This was 1996, after all.)

I don't remember whether I thought my parents were cool when I was a kid. I was convinced they didn't understand me, of course, but these days I look back on that feeling and think they were better off. I was a weird kid, and I spent a frighteningly high percentage of my teen years in my bedroom writing bad stories or daydreaming about dating Gene Wilder.

One day I realized that, even if my mother herself wasn't cool (and really, she was—our house was one of the "hangout" houses for me and my friends), her *job* was cool. I wish I hadn't taken it for granted back then, because it was downright awesome to have a parent who worked at the Crayola factory.

Yes, if you haven't worked up a big batch of envy toward me before this point in the book, now's your chance. My mother worked where they make Crayola crayons ... and markers ... and poster paint ... and glue ... and flash cards (well, okay, maybe not so much envy for the flash cards) ... and (drum roll, please) ... wait for it, wait for it ... *Silly Putty*.

Back in the dark ages of the late '70s, the Crayola company bought the Silly Putty brand and began manufacturing it themselves. By this point, my mother worked in the Quality Control department, having worked her way up from various stations in the crayon department. I'm not quite sure how you work your way up through the crayon department: Perhaps you start out with the eight basic colors of crayons, then graduate to the 24-box for a while.

Once you've mastered that, you're allowed into the inner sanctum of Burnt Sienna and Periwinkle. Eventually, they let you work on the 64-box—the one with the splendiferous built-in crayon sharpener—before allowing you to load up the Crayola Caddy or fold the flash cards. And then, when you least expect it, you're shown the secret world of Quality Control.

And that's where my mother's story gets really interesting. So, wake up.

Testing Crayola products all day—for money—seems a lot like the job Tom Hanks had in the movie *Big*, testing toys. Oh sure, my mother had to test the products for various incremental differences in quality—the thickness of the plastic trays, the quality and glue on the crayon labels, the wax-to-color ratio of the crayons themselves—but she also got to play with the stuff.

And the coolest stuff she got to play with has to be the Silly Putty. She had a line on a wall of her office, at about the six-foot mark. It reminded me of the way parents make marker-lines on the kitchen doorway to measure their children's growth over the years. But this six-foot mark served one purpose: My mother balled up an egg's worth of Silly Putty and bounced it on the floor, watching to see if it bounced up to that six-foot line on her wall.

Now, that's a job I want.

But, it gets better. Crayola also made glow-in-the-dark Silly Putty. That stuff had to not only bounce six feet in the air, but it had to, well ... it had to, umm... okay, it had to glow in the dark. (You saw that coming, didn't you?) Sparing no expense, Crayola supplied my mother with a shoe box with a small hole cut into the lid and a desk lamp. (You can see where this is going, can't you? Don't spoil it for the others.)

She'd hold that glow-in-the-dark Putty under her desk lamp for a predetermined amount of time (I'm fuzzy on the specifics here—I was only sixteen, after all, and had more important things to remember, like Gene Wilder's birthday), then quickly popped it into the shoe box and closed the lid. She'd peer through the hole in the lid and decide whether it was, well... umm... whether it was glowing. In the dark.

And people wondered why the Crayola employees never felt the need to unionize...

Having a parent with a cool job doesn't really hit home with most teens unless, well... umm... unless it hits home. My mom's job hit home with a vengeance. You see, she often brought home a few crayons here or there—the ones she'd tested and couldn't put back on the line for customers. We never lacked for art supplies. But one day we hit the mother lode.

What happens when an entire batch of Silly Putty is found to be slightly defective? And, I mean, slightly? Enough to take it off the line of production, but not enough to really damage any of its basic properties? Of course, it comes home to our house. All five pounds of it. All six cubic feet of it. In a big plastic bag. Inside a heavy unmarked cardboard box.

My brother and I kept that gargantuan slab of Silly Putty in the closet in the dining room for years. We had more Silly Putty than twenty kids would know what to do with. There weren't enough comics pages in the world to get through that Silly Putty. And bouncing it in the kitchen? It actually got boring after a while.

I have no idea how we kept using and losing bits and pieces of it and yet always seemed to have the same amount in that secret cardboard box. It never seemed to run out. It was like our own personal sourdough starter.

After my mother retired and I had children of my own, I saw a Silly Putty egg in the store and bought one for my kids. I explained how awesome it had been to plaster huge hunks of the stuff onto whole pages of comics when I was a kid, so I could stretch the faces out and laugh. My children beamed with excitement...

...Until we opened the egg and found a tiny wedge of Silly Putty the size of my fingernail. My pinky fingernail.

My children learned a harsh life-lesson that day. So did I. I had taken my mother's hard work for granted all those years earlier. Most children had to suffer with infinitesimal bits of Silly Putty while my brother and I hoarded a block of Silly Putty the size of Rhode Island.

Life isn't fair, my children. It's best if you get used to it early. The size of the Silly Putty in that egg is the least of your worries.

Attack of the 50-Square-Foot Bathroom (Day 273)

We've made a list of things we still have to finish on the eternal bathroom project. Every time we cross one thing off, we add three more. And when I say "we," I mean "Wayne." I have a vested interest in the success of this project—if only because I own a pair of functioning kidneys and I get sweaty and dirty just like normal people—but at this point, any inkling that I've ever been a perfectionist has gone right out the window along with two old sinks, a toilet, and twenty-seven pieces of glass block. I don't care if nothing matches and nothing is plumb or level. I just want my bathroom back. I have, though, long since stopped taking bets. I'm a lousy gambler.

When I look at our to-do list—which Wayne keeps on an ever-growing spreadsheet on his computer—I want to join the Boy Scouts, learn how to tie proper knots, and make myself a noose. When Wayne looks at our to-do list—which now needs its own terrabyte hard drive—he thinks, "This project isn't big enough yet."

Or at least, I assume that's what he's thinking, based on how many more tasks he's added along the way. Let's not just put in that cool one-piece vinyl flooring that fooled my daughter into thinking it was real tile. No, let's put in actual white octagonal tiles the size of my pinky that will take a decade to grout properly. Let's not just put in white octagonal tiles the size of my pinky. No, let's create a pattern of small black tiles around the entire edge of the room and black-tile diamond patterns under each of the four ceiling lights.

If I didn't know better, I'd swear he was having a snow-piddling contest with himself to see how many tools and raw supplies he can use on a single bathroom. Oh wait, I probably *don't* know better.

In the past thirty-nine weeks (which is dangerously close to how long it takes to *grow an entire human being from scratch*), we've learned a lot, most of it the hard way. We've learned that it doesn't really save money to buy generic blue painter's tape, unless you don't mind a strange scritchy blue "pattern" along the edges where the shower meets the wall ... and the wall meets the vanity ... and the vanity meets the other wall ... and the window meets the wainscoting ...

We've learned that taking a week's vacation time to finish the project will be a great idea ... sometime next decade once the only thing we have left to do is put the knobs on the vanity drawers.

We've also learned that time waits for no man. We don't really know what that means, but it really feels true. And bad. It really feels bad. Which is why it really feels true.

I had decided months ago to start taking notes on the parts of this project that are humorous, so that I can include an essay about it in my next book. At first, I was scribbling notes so fast I was giddy with all the new material Wayne was providing for me every time he swung a hammer or couldn't get the stud finder to work. ("Can't find any studs? I'm right here!")

But after the day counter went well past three digits, and climbed up over 200, suddenly nothing was funny anymore. Suddenly, the little notebook in which I was scrawling my notes began collecting dust. And I don't mean drywall dust. I kept telling myself I'd pick my pen back up as soon as something funny happened. The ink in the pen dried up before that happened.

After learning so many wonderful new things about remodeling a bathroom from the outer walls in, we turn to each other and say, "Never again!"

And then, we buy a new house that needs renovation work in only *one ... single ... room ...*

About the Author

(Linda's Life in a Nutshell ... where it belongs)

In the early 1980s, Linda pursued a writing degree from Carnegie Mellon University in Pittsburgh, Pa. She pursued it but it kept getting away.

She has since worked behind the scenes in publishing as a proofreader, typesetter and copyeditor. She's worked with publishers, big and small, and with individual authors, big and small. (The big ones really ought to get a little more exercise.) She's also an 8th grade writing coach for the online writing curriculum at WriteAtHome.com.

Linda is currently on the board of the St. Davids Christian Writers' Association. She also serves as author liaison for the Beaver County BookFest in Beaver,

Pennsylvania. She sounds really important and busy, doesn't she? She's not, but it's still a shame she doesn't get paid for any of these things.

Her favorite writing challenge since 2004 has been the yearly contest known as National Novel Writing Month: writing 50,000 words of a single new fiction project during the month of November. She loves the pressure of a ridiculous, forced deadline.

Linda also enjoys comedy, computer gadgets, office supplies, reading, movies, adventure games, crocheting—and her office guinea pigs, who keep her company while she's working. She currently lives in western Pennsylvania with her husband, Wayne Parker. They share six children between them, all of them now grown and living their own humorous stories.

www.ingramcontent.com/pod-product-compliance
Lightning Source LLC
Chambersburg PA
CBHW060742050426
42449CB00008B/1286

9781954973046